Who Says It's Over

A fading child star's humorous and compelling true
story about gambling, life-threatening encounters
and a remarkable journey back to
Hollywood prominence.

A Memoir

by

Joseph Walsh

www.josephrwalsh.com
www.whosaysitsover.com

For my wonderful children: Kelly, Josie,
Kathryn, and Ryan..
and for 'Lights', my wife and partner
in all things.

Acknowledgments

To Barbara (Lights) Lightstone, whose keen eye,
encouragement, and contributions are woven
throughout these pages. Can't possibly
thank her enough;

To Patti and Howard Lightstone, whose generosity
in time, ideas, and patience were a constant.
Much much gratitude.

It takes some work, a bit of luck, and a whole lot of grace to go beyond yourself; but stay open to it. It is well worth it.

Table of Contents

Foreword

Who Says It's Over is the authentic and inspired story
of my friend, Joseph Raymond Walsh. Joey could do
anything and do it well. He was smart, tough, and
gifted and would gamble and bet on everything.
Playing stickball on the street, baseball in the park,
ping pong, bowling, cards, taking the points or laying
the odds, he loved the action. From his dream of being
a boxer (and he could fight) to acting in Hollywood with
the greats including Kirk Douglas, Frank Sinatra,
Gregory Peck, Robert Mitchum and Danny Kaye. He
kept himself alive with his skill and competitive spirit.
He once wrote to me that things were so tough in the
acting business that even Bambi had to take a job
playing *The Yearling* in summer stock. Eventually, he
realized that he'd have to do something different and
not just depend on acting and gambling. So, he wrote
his own movie, *California Split* (considered to be one of
the best movies about gambling) and produced it with
the great Robert Altman, who also directed it.

Who Says It's Over is a kaleidoscope and gold mine
about a one of a kind human being.

A bold and resourceful player and an indefatigable
spirit you gotta love.

Elliott Gould

Introduction

In 2018, I was at a memorial for a friend, and got into 'small talk' with a theatrical agent I hadn't seen in many years. Nothing deep, so the energy that ensued was of low wattage. Just a courtesy of interest that would evaporate in a matter of minutes. Things picked up though when my beloved wife stepped in to answer the question, 'was I still writing?' She talked up some pages I had written due to a phone call from actor George Segal. Seems like George had been telling my Billy The Kid story for a number of years, which had regaled his listeners, and thought I should write it down and give it to some magazine.

This was only a one or two page incident at most, and couldn't see why any magazine would want to publish it. George said elongate it and I said with what? He didn't know, but why not give it a try. I gave him an okay, which was a maybe, heading for a no.

Somewhere along the line I picked up a pen. First it was six pages, then ten, fourteen, and George kept pushing for more because he was loving it that much. That kind of zeal doesn't come along that often, so he had me where he wanted me. It ended up at thirty pages, at which point he promptly sent it off to his friend, director Terrence Malick, who in turn sent it off to David Remnick, editor of the New Yorker Magazine.

Remnick had nothing but high praise for the material, but unfortunately it was much too long a piece to fit into the New Yorker format.

Hey, no harm, no foul. Now it had to go into deep hibernation, where if needed again, the chance of me ever finding it would be an all day affair, stretching out to possibly never. Luckily, I was married to a woman who could find anything within thirteen seconds. This particular piece she found in five, then sent it off to the agent, convinced that once he read it he would see it's commercial possibilities. He did: 'New York street kid becomes reluctant child star...interacts with famous people...faces career slide...turns into gambling guru... attracts the Hollywood wagering elite...faces death...writes classic movie...and for extras, experiences reincarnation. The agent was sold with one request. Additional pages. A lot more. Full out memoir.

Nice that the agent and my wife were excited, but where was I in this process? I hadn't picked up a pen in years, and I wasn't so anxious for a showdown with the written word again. Not that I'd run out of ink, but these face-offs took a lot of energy, and I wasn't sure I was up to the task. More motivation was needed and I found it via my children.

Back where I grew up on the East side of New York, kids like me were seriously into stickball and a good scrap not words like 'Hey mom, dad, tell me your life story because I can't sleep until I know everything.' Unfortunately, I never did get around to asking them much of anything, so after they were gone, that felt like a loss.

Certainly my kids knew more about me than I knew about my parents, but here I was being given the opportunity to fill in the 'who am I' part in full detail. This question was not new to me. Once upon a fateful time, a big time movie director supposedly wanted to know the same thing when he said, "So tell me about yourself?" On it's face, an innocent enough query. But within seconds I was inches away of ending an already floundering career, and likely to be serving jail time. I'll get to that later, but for now let's just believe there was an angel on my shoulder.

Back when I was a street-smart kid who thought he knew everything, I didn't need anybody, including angels. Basically my attitude was—C'mon world, show me what ya got, and I'll see what I do about it. Oh, and just a word of caution…better not get too out of line or you'll hear from me.

Not that I was the toughest kid in the world, far from it. Being headstrong was just ingrained in my DNA, and definitely posed a problem to my physical well being. All in all, I wasn't complicated. A pretty straightforward 'so that happened' kinda guy. Don't push and we'll get along just fine. Good chance we'll even have some laughs along the way. Life belonged to me and I knew just what I wanted from it…<u>Become welterweight champion.</u>

But in between what you want and what you get is why we tell each other stories. Here's mine.

"Alright, Make Me Him"

"He can play trouble…That's his specialty," so said the producer to director Sidney Lumet. The year was 1951. The series was called DANGER. The episode was entitled 'Death Among The Relics', and at age thirteen, I was about to become the hottest child actor in early live New York television. So popular was this particular show, the city demanded I do the exact same episode one year later. An unheard of event at the time. While my father was skipping for joy, I could barely catch my breath under the workload that followed. How the hell did life as a fun loving street kid vanish so quickly? For the answer, lets fade back three years earlier where this little scene was taking place.

He whacked me again on the back of my ten-year-old head and bellowed, "What are you—a fuckin' idiot?! If you're looking to get punched around for a living, look no further 'cause I'm your guy!!"

With that came a double head thumping. Back in the day, this is what passed for fatherly love. Of course being an East-side kid with plenty of moxie, I wasn't taking all this 'affection' lying down. I was still getting in my licks—only verbally.

"G'won," he said, "keep offering up the lip and I'll fatten it for you."

Even though my father was a big fight fan, catching his kid boxing in the gym, secretly training to become the next Sugar Ray Robinson (my idol), drove him absolutely nuts. I couldn't seem to convince him that he was interfering with greatness. I had it all. I was fast. I could punch. I was fearless. Seventy-six pounds of pugilistic fury who was destined to become the welterweight champ. All the way home he 'showered' me with love in his effort to convince me otherwise.

As far as he was concerned, my hands were made for the piano. Since I possessed great speed, my father was certain if I could play Frederic Chopin's Minute Waltz faster than anybody else, dead or alive, it would be my ticket to fame and fortune. Every day he would be after me to get it faster and faster. He even bought a stopwatch just like the ones that time race horses.

He would always say, "You're on the clock. Go!"

And off my little fingers went in breakneck speed. Still, my best time was one minute and seventeen seconds. I couldn't imagine my frenzied fingers moving a second faster, let alone seventeen to reach the fabled one minute mark. Dad believed otherwise, and that's all that mattered to him. I often thought of stealing his stopwatch and throwing it down a sewer, but knew he'd suspect me and just buy another, so why start a riot.

During this period, I was selected, along with ten other gifted young pianists, to play an afternoon recital at the world famous Carnegie Hall. Each pianist would have two pieces to perform. Mine were both by Chopin: Polonaise in A Flat Major, and the Minute Waltz. When the recital was over, my father was ecstatic. He couldn't care less that I did an inspired job on the Polonaise, because he was beside himself that I had broken my record. Played the Minute Waltz in a minute and fifteen!

The music director approached me shortly thereafter and said he'd never witnessed anyone play the Minute Waltz at such speed. He seemed genuinely surprised. Feeling pretty good, I told him it hadn't been easy, and who knows, unless my fingers fell off, maybe I could chop off a few more seconds in the near future. Then came the grim facts. He told me Chopin meant the piece to be played at a good clip, but definitely not at a berserk pace. Ideally, it should be played between 90 to 120 seconds. In actuality, Chopin conceived the Minute (mi-nūte) Waltz in terms of 'small'. Not the Minute Waltz in terms of 'time'.

This news landed heavily on dad, who ceremoniously crushed his stopwatch and fired my piano teacher. Poor Dad. Now that his dream was shattered, he was a shell of himself. Perfect. Make room for glory. It wasn't longer than a New York minute before I was back at the gym, deftly out-boxing some dude who had a good forty pounds on me. I was in heaven, when in walked dad, back from the dead. There he was, fully recovered, and back in slap-happy mode with the side of my head.

Just before we reached home, my father, either arm-weary or feeling bad about inflicting possible brain damage said, "Look kid, it gives me no pleasure hitting you 'cause you know I love you, right?" (It's good he didn't wait for an answer.) "So you better believe I'm dead serious when I tell you, I'll be damned before I'd ever let you become some fuckin' punch drunk, cauliflower-eared shitty pug, wandering around queer street. Better I should march you up to the top of this building, throw you off the fuckin' roof and save us all a lot of misery."

I could handle the roof part, but the word shitty really pissed me off. That's how much he knew about my sneaky-but-lethal left hook.

"I'll make you anything else you wanna be. Anything. Just name it, you got it."

So with as much arrogance as I could muster, pointed to the marquee of our local RKO theater, where a child actor named Dean Stockwell was starring in a movie called THE BOY WITH THE GREEN HAIR, and said, "Alright, make me him". I knew my father couldn't deliver such a thing, giving me some small measure of satisfaction. Sure, he worked on Broadway—but as a sight-seeing guide, not some movie producer. Besides, who ever thought about becoming an actor? Certainly not me.

Those flippant four words - 'alright make me him' - carried more weight than I could have imagined. Whether by chance or some 'higher cosmic power' leading the way, things would never be the same.

Quicker than Willie Pep's jab, my father brought me to meet a man named John Ross, who was anxious to be in show business. He had an easy going style about him that felt different than anyone I knew from the East Side. Said he recently returned from the Arctic and had brought back a penguin, which was kept in his bathtub on blocks of ice. The penguin seemed to be loving New York, he added, but keeled over dead after seven days. He felt genuinely bad about that. I didn't feel too good about the demise of the penguin, but you don't run into a story like that everyday. I was impressed. So he became my manager—whatever that meant?

After giving me a month of acting lessons, and learning a few dance routines from his girlfriend, we were set to go. At that time, many movie theaters throughout the boroughs of New York would have a talent contest between movie showings. Went to four of them, won first prize in all and picked up ten to fifteen bucks. Besides playing the Minute Waltz, and doing a comic dance routine, I did a short monologue about Skippy the dog, who'd been run over by a garbage truck. This would always propel me into crying like a fool each and every time I performed it. I was always a big animal lover, so maybe that's why it triggered a waterfall of emotion.

As it turned out, the 'combo special' I was serving up proved to be irresistible. The violinists, harpists, acrobats, opera singers, etc., didn't stand a chance. I was convinced Skippy, the road-kill dog, and the real tears delivered the dagger to the heart of the competition. I can't say I liked doing the talent shows that much, but enjoyed winning because my manager and his girlfriend always bought me a whole cantaloupe filled with vanilla ice cream. If I had to miss stickball games by doing this junk, a payoff of some kind was required or forget it. Who needed this?

Being an undefeated talent show winner, led me to something called Stars and Starters, where each contestant would be presented by a star in their chosen field. Motion picture star, Arlene Dahl, would be my sponsor in the acting category. She was so beautiful, my little heart was all aflutter. I couldn't care less about winning the $25 war bond, or the promise of potential future stardom. All I wanted to do was come through for the gorgeous Arlene Dahl, so I pushed Skippy, the dead dog to inspired new heights. I was blubbering for all I was worth, and won first prize going away. My darling Arlene was so proud of me, all thoughts of cantaloupe and vanilla ice cream vanished from my mind. She wasn't married at that time, so there was a chance. Until then, I never realized I was such a romantic.

After my moment of bliss cooled down, nothing much happened for awhile until I auditioned for the Dumont Television Network when TV was so new, nobody in my entire neighborhood owned a set. The year was 1949, and I landed the role of the family idiot in a show called *The Family Genius*. Word traveled quickly that I was a natural, and when that show ended, CBS and NBC came a calling, casting me in practically everything they had to offer. My Catholic school definitely wasn't thrilled with me missing so many classes because of TV commitments; but when I smacked a nun's hat ass-backward, they felt compelled to expel.

When I got the boot, I explained to my incredulous father that I never minded Sister Irwin taking a ruler to the palm of my hand on a regular basis. But pulling little Esther's pigtail much too often was a no go, and I told her so. This naturally led to extra whacks for me, and unfortunately no let up in pigtail pulling. Dad knew Sister Irwin was considered the meanest person on earth, complete with villainous mustache, so I figured he would cut me some slack on my actions. After all, he was far from a holier-than-thou Catholic. He used a ton of foul language on a daily basis, and consumed as much meat on Fridays as his false teeth could hold.

Still, he couldn't get over the idea of me hitting a nun.

Mom jumped to my defense, "He cuffed the hat, and as far as I'm concerned, she had it coming."

Mom was always my super support system. Being eternally positive, she always felt that since I entered the world on 7/11, the stars were aligned in my favor. I didn't know about that stuff, but maybe she was right on some level, because I always had confidence things would work out just fine. Definitely picked up that quality from her. Dad, on the other hand, was run more by his fearful side; constantly after me to do things his way. Because we were so different, this was bound to cause friction.

Thirty Broken Noses

Upon expulsion from Catholic school, Dad took a decidedly different interest in me as he hand delivered me to Professional Children's School (P.C.S.), located on 61st and Broadway. Being escorted to a fancy school was quite the change. What made this a little weird, especially the personal service part by Dad, was the fact that at age nine, I would trudge through rain and blizzards for five long New York city blocks all by my lonesome to Holly's bakery. There I would get my usual coffee and six small heated jelly donuts, before heading down toward the East River and Catholic school. In today's world, that could have been considered child endangerment, along with an arrest warrant for Dad.

For me, I didn't know what the big fuss was over show business. Taking care of myself was never a problem before. Dad's final warning to me when we reached my new school was…"This is important, so stay the hell out of trouble."

Easier said than done. My first day at P.C.S. came close to being my last. For some reason, I was a pen collector. Strange, because I wasn't at all interested in writing, rarely ever doing homework. Yet here I arrive at this private school with my fifty-two what-for-pens. After returning from school lunch, and a nerve-racking encounter with my first salad, I wasn't in the best of moods. SO--whoever thought breaking all my pens in half, was a funny opening, better be talking real fast. I looked around for clues. A lot of very pretty girls were nervously glancing toward a very tall, pudgy kid with a shit-eating grin. This was definitely culprit material. Everything about him fit the picture. The size...The silly arrogance...The heft.

As pen-breakers go, he was pretty impressive. But that didn't stop me. Thanks to my neighborhood buddies, I was used to fighting guys bigger and stronger than me. If they got hit by anybody more sizable than them, I would be first call to deliver payback. Not that I asked for the job, but since I apparently had taken on thirty guys single-handedly, and broken everyone's nose, they made me their designated bully-buster. The only thing missing from that 'glorified story' was me riding off in a Chariot, with garlands of flowers being thrown. What really happened was dramatic enough for me, but far from the crap that was floating around.

I had heard there was a stickball game in progress at a nearby neighborhood, and anything stickball, say no more, I'm on my way. Much to my disappointment, when I got there the game was over. A few guys were milling around, and one kid in particular was voicing off with such profanity, it bothered me. Because of my father's foul language one might think I was used to it,

24

but this kid's crudeness really got to me. I should have dismissed it and walked. Instead I said, "Hey, is it possible for you to say anything without using a curse word?"

"Fuck off, cocksucker," he instantly replied, and just as instantly I slapped him, taking things further than it should have gone.

He immediately told me to wait right there, because he's going to get his older brother after me. I was steamed now, both at myself and the kid, and said, "G'won, get anybody you want." Saying that meant I had to stay, because the thought of me running away was out of the question. But I certainly wasn't looking forward to what could take place, that's for sure. Twenty minutes later, I'm about to leave, when here comes a mob of guys. Shit. Why couldn't I have passed the courage test one minute earlier? Too late now. Stand tall. Show no fear. Think fast.

Marching straight up to me, some hard-faced kid says, "Did you slap my brother?" Without hesitation I told him I had, because he's got a dirty little mouth, and maybe being his older brother, he should do something about it. Menacingly he says, that's what we are here to do. I knew the word 'we' meant the big gang beatdown was about to take place, so my best bet was to embarrass them from an all out attack.

"Oh, what a bunch of tough guys you are. You cowards need an army to take on just one guy? Ha, what a group of lowly COWARDS." This stopped the older brother cold, like I hoped it would.

"Seacliff," he yelled!

With that, their hulk enforcer moved through the horde to be my sole combatant. One guy! Already I was ahead of the game. However, Seacliff had a look of a guy who could break me in half, so there wasn't a second to lose. I stunned the crowd by blasting him the moment he approached. Hit him with the best shot I had, which landed square on his nose, turning it into something that looked like the letter S.

Next thing I know he's tackling me to the ground. It was like having a two-ton truck on top of me. No matter how hard I tried, I was unable to budge him. While bleeding all over me, he kept saying, "Do you give up...Do you give up...Do you give up?"

Eventually I said, "I'm not going to lie on the ground all day long with you, so yeah, ok, you win. I give up." With that, the fight was over. He let me up and I didn't waste a moment. Looking as defeated as the situation called for, I left with my head slumped down. I was smart enough to know that if I gave them any amount of time to think, it wouldn't turn out well for me. I didn't want to be around when they figured out I had escaped

26

without a scratch. Yet…somehow I had acquired super hero status following this incident. I actually met a guy who insisted what he heard about thirty broken noses was true, even though I kept telling him it wasn't. Unbelievable. I was there, he wasn't, and here he is arguing with me about the facts. He just didn't seem to like the real story that featured 'guile over brawn'. Fine, I told him, have it your way. That's how a 'fish tale' became East Side lore.

The pen-buster certainly wasn't a Seacliff, but it didn't matter what his size. I walked straight up to this kid and asked if he was the one who broke all my pens. With amazing pride he said 'yeah', and that's all she wrote.

Fifteen minutes later, being viewed as a wild street ruffian who struck an upstanding professional child, I was set to be expelled from a second school in less than a week. But thanks to all the girls in the class, who seemed more than happy to tell the principal what had happened, I was exonerated. For these particular female thespians, being rough around the edges seemed to carry some movie gangster appeal.

As one wide-eyed young lovely told me, her father's favorite actor was James Cagney and that I reminded her of him. This carried quite an impact, because only a day before I had gone to see a revival of the movie, *Public Enemy*. It had made Cagney a star and I loved every minute of it, except for the ending. After being fatally shot, Cagney looks up to the heavens and utters, "I ain't so tough." Then falls face down dead in the rainy gutter. I felt heartsick.

As I left the movie house, it started to rain and remember thinking as much as I liked Cagney, I didn't want to end up like that. I don't know why such a thought would enter my head, but maybe my psyche was picking something up, because I would come real close on later occasions.

At the present though, playtime was becoming a distant memory. I was 'it' when it came to child actors. Thanks a lot Mister Lumet for casting me as that misunderstood, dead-end kid.

Because of it, writers of all kind were creating stories with just me in mind. Somebody should have broken their pens—and I knew just the right kid for the job, and it wasn't the other kid—who, by the way, was sent home from school for two whole days for breaking my pens. Boy, what torture. If that is what crime and punishment looked like, better keep an eye on me.

Saying No to Sam Goldwyn

As jobs poured in fast and furious, I struggled to keep up with the demand. Rushing from one rehearsal to another, to do two different live shows a week, was really getting to me. If you were a child whose talent wasn't much in demand, you had a lot of free time, and a real shot at passing a test. I wasn't in that category. When it came to math class and social studies, I was usually at NBC or CBS yelling, "Back off coppers…I'm holding Nitroglycerin in my hand!"

The public loved it. Couldn't get enough of my bad behavior. They even awarded me a gold star for all my troubles. It certainly was a dream come true for my father, but a clear disappointment for a lot of jealous stage mothers. They grouped together and called the Child Labor Board demanding a stop to the abuse of a minor. Basically to give their kid more chances to be equally abused. Even my manager lamented the fact that he didn't have five more of me. It was a light bulb moment.

Somehow I thought that more competition would add up to less work, and that couldn't come soon enough. Being directed around a maze of taped flooring (representing the set) doing make believe hour after hour, felt like forced slave camp. I longed for the unstructured ease of being a neighborhood kid, playing stickball to my heart's delight. So in self-defense, I quickly got to my manager and talked up a feisty Irish kid who lived across the street from me.

I had no idea if the kid would be interested in acting, but I knew his family were basically 'brokos' like the rest of the neighborhood. Maybe even more so, because he lived with a single mom and kid sister. Definitely worth a shot. So my manager came down, pitched the kid and his mom about letting him become an actor, but ran into an unexpected snag. The little kid sister. My manager didn't want her, just the boy. He finally relented to a pleading, tear-filled mom. The boy went on to work in television. The little kid sister didn't do so bad herself. His name was Raymond Duke. Her name was Patty Duke, who went on to win an Academy Award. Fascinating how the world has 'miracles' up its sleeve that we never could have imagined.

The thing I figured out, was that my father feared I might team up with the rival parents, and squeal on myself for working too much. It was smart of him to buy me off with ten bucks a show. Even though I wasn't thrilled with acting, I must admit I did like the dough. So when Hollywood came a calling, all I could see were dollar signs. I immediately started negotiating with my father. My ten buck a show had to be upped to a hundred, because I was bound to make millions if I got the job.

The facts were that Samuel Goldwyn was going to make his most expensive movie ever—a musical about the life of *Hans Christian Andersen*, starring Danny Kaye. Word was they had searched the world for six months, looking for the right boy to play the part of Peter, Danny's sweet, lovable sidekick in the movie. Naturally that led them to the New York delinquent with the sneaky-but-lethal left hook.

They arranged a screen test in some dumpy warehouse in the Bronx, where they dressed me up in a Danish boy outfit and asked me questions. Toughies like.. What was my name.. Where was I born.. Did I have any hobbies, etc. Certainly not ground breaking material, but I guess I was lucky they didn't ask me to recite the big 'to be or not to be' speech from *Hamlet*. Still, it was supposed to be a major Hollywood screen test, so you would think they might have pressed me for more drama. Something like-"Hey Hans, are you kidding with these friggin' wooden shoes. They're killing my feet." Anyway, I knew my name and where I lived and hopefully that wowed them, because I was still thinking humongous Hollywood money.

After two months, my dreams of making the big score

were all but gone. Hollywood never called. At this point, moments away from signing for my first Broadway Show, my manager decided to step into a phone booth and call the Sam Goldwyn people to inform them I was no longer available. This was being done strictly as a joke, to show Hollywood I didn't need them as much as they didn't need me. When he got off the phone, he was speechless. It seemed I was due in Hollywood the following day. I had landed the biggest and most sought after role in Tinseltown, but someone at the studio forgot to call us about it. Shocking as this was, it was even more shocking when we turned them down.

The land where the gold rush started, offered me $250 a week to star with Danny Kaye in this big musical extravaganza. We were dumbfounded. I was making $500 a week in lowly TV. It didn't make any sense! Of course, to Goldwyn it made perfect sense. As the story goes, he screamed at the top of his lungs, "I can't work with idiots! Here I am offering him the break of a lifetime and the idiots say no! They should be paying me $250 to let him play the role!!"

After three weeks of silence on the studio's part, everybody we knew in New York came to agree with Goldwyn—we were idiots. It seemed ironic that I started out my career playing the idiot, and would end it by becoming one. Then to an idiot's delight, Goldwyn called and made a final offer of $400 a week. Like geniuses, we said—Now you're talking.

Danny Kaye vs. Street Kid

For an East Side kid who had never been anywhere out of the area, traveling to Hollywood on the legendary Super Chief train was like being in Wonderland. From plush sleeping quarters, to exotic-lit lounge areas, to glorious Irish linen clad dining tables, to high society clientele. The grandeur never stopped. I kept waiting for someone to grab me by the back of my collar and say, 'How the hell did you sneak aboard.' Even the silverware was unfair. So spectacularly ornate, I had to stop my mother from slipping a spoon into her purse. For days I never ate, slept, or indulged myself more. Maybe this show business wasn't so bad after all.

Stepping off the train was another whole trip. Millions of popping flash bulbs made it difficult to see who was taking them. Turned out to be Samuel Goldwyn's publicity department. Seemed like I was a big deal to them, so I gave them the old Hollywood wave. They loved it. When they wearied of picture taking, which seemed like never, a publicist whisked me right off to Goldwyn's movie studio, where I was taken to the office of Samuel Goldwyn's wife. She was talking on the phone in a thick back-east accent, and just lit up when she saw me.

"Oh Ethel, he just arrived wearing this yella sweater. So adorable. I can't stand it."

After a few minutes of whatever we talked about, she gave me a big hug, and off I went to another office meet. As we approached the door, the publicist shushed me, even though I hadn't said a word. When he knocked, a gruff voice yelled to come in. We entered to a man, cigarette in mouth, tinkering out a song on the piano.

The publicist pointed at me proudly and said, "Our Peter."

Piano man grinned. "Leave him with me for a few minutes."

As the publicist was leaving, the piano man motioned for me to come sit on the piano bench with him. Soon as I was seated, he immediately started playing and singing:

> "Thumbelina, Thumbelina, tiny little thing.
> Thumbelina dance, Thumbelina sing.
> Thumbelina, what's the difference
> If you're very small?
> When your heart is full of love,
> you're nine feet tall."

Finishing, he turned and asked, "Cute? Corny? What?"

I liked the rhyme and went with the word, "Fun."

He smiled. "What's wrong with fun?"

"Nothing," I replied.

"Great," he said, "the song stays in the picture." With that he stuck out his hand and said, "Good to meet you, Peter. I'm Frank Loesser." A year prior, Mr. Loesser had written the words and music to the hit musical *Guys & Dolls.*

I didn't meet Danny Kaye until the first day of shooting, where he started right off becoming competitive with me. Moments before we were about to do our first scene, he started to tell me about his amazing foot speed. He was fast as a Whippet. Could spot me ten yards and run me down in a flash. At the time I didn't know what a Whippet was, but it sure sounded fast. Didn't matter. I was always up for a challenge, so the race was on. No doubt Danny was fast, but I left the Whippet part of him in the dust.

For close to a half-hour, he pursued me relentlessly down cobblestones streets, over moats, past bridges, through push-car vendors, scattering goats, geese, chickens, you name it, in every panicked direction.

Basically all through the largest and most expensive set ever built in Hollywood at the time. It would have cost less to film it in Copenhagen rather than build the whole city, but this was Goldwyn's baby and he wanted the sound and everything else to be picture perfect.

I'm sure if and when he found out his dollars were flying out the window on an ego-driven foot race, he wouldn't be too happy. Neither was the 'Whippet' when he finally quit in a fallen heap. A wise move on Mr. Kaye's part, because he had a better chance of getting a heart-attack than he had of catching me.

The sweet feeling of victory didn't last long. Round 2 took place a few days later, and I wasn't on the winning side. There's a scene in *Andersen* where I have to eat a slice of rye bread lathered in sour cream. Wincing at the first taste of it was like committing the cardinal mistake. Kaye's eyes widened mischievously. Shit! Never let your opponent see your weakness. I knew I was in for it.

The Whippet took his revenge. Take after take, he would deliberately blow his last line, so we had to do the thing over and over. I was fighting nausea as my stomach rebelled, but I wouldn't give him the satisfaction of throwing up. My mother knew exactly what was happening and threatened to hit Danny if he messed up one more time. He feigned innocence and mock fearfulness, while trying to stifle his inner delight.

(Still to this day, when TV plays the movie during holidays, I cringe at the sour cream moment.)

We filmed for eight long months and I'm convinced that the nature of our friendly but 'intense rivalry' added at least a month to the shoot. There was never a dull moment. I take that back. Danny Kaye singing INCH WORM hour after hour, while I'm supposedly staring at an inchworm, was my equivalent of being waterboarded. Although I never let on. In fact, I told him I really liked doing that scene, hoping that would convince him to complete it. He did. Chalk one up for me.

Taking on the Sea of Galilee

During the final week of filming *Hans Christian Andersen*, I was anxious to get back to New York. However, my Hollywood representative from the William Morris Agency came by to say he had another movie lined up for me. It would require me to leave for Israel the moment I finished *Andersen*.

For most actors, this would have been terrific news, but to me it was a bummer. Mostly due to a girl I had just met before coming to California. When saying our goodbyes, her eyes had filled with tears. Up till then I had only seen this happen in movies, and boy was it effective. Even though I'd only known her approximately 39 hours, the romantic in me stirred, and I wanted to rise to the occasion by telling her something like…'this would be the last time I would ever be leaving her.' While it's true we weren't exactly Ingrid and Bogie from *Casablanca,* I wasn't too pleased with my father's comment.

"What are you, a complete sap. There's still plenty of fish in the ocean."

I don't know how a remark referring to you as a moron is supposed to make you feel any better, but it was the best dad had to offer. Still, I held out hope the movie deal would fall through. It depended on big name producer Stanley Kramer, seeing some footage of me in *Andersen*. The good news came when Samuel Goldwyn turned down Kramer's request, refusing to show him anything. The bad news came when Stanley Kramer basically said to Goldwyn, screw you, because I'm hiring him anyway. So sight unseen, one day after completing work on *Andersen,* I was on a plane flying off to Israel at a salary of six hundred bucks a week. It was the first American movie to be filmed in the Holy Land. This made a lot of people jump for joy—except for me.

After eight months of being the sidekick to Hans Christian Andersen, I was to be the sidekick to another 'Hans'. Instead of it being serial competitor, Danny Kaye, this time it would be sidekick to Kirk Douglas, playing Hans Muller, a psychologically disturbed man in a movie called *The Juggler*. Playing a sidekick for two Han's in a row, had to be a movie first, and hopefully for me, a last.

The best thing about the trip is that it made my mom happy.

Every time the stewardess/flight attendant walked past, my mom would tell her very excitedly, "We're going to Israel..We're going to Israel." To which the pretty, green-eyed lady responded, "I know..I know..Tell your son to smile." That was always followed by a wink from her and a nudge from Mom. They were having a good time at my refusal to smile. I felt I owed the sour face to the poor girl back home who was undoubtedly pining away for me. When we stepped off the plane in Israel, all thoughts of heartbreak vanished quickly. Staying alive now, became the topic at hand.

The airport was surrounded by armed Israeli troops, looking deadly serious. Seems the night before there had been an Arab attack on the site, resulting in many deaths. Certainly a comforting feeling as we're about to embark on a two and a half hour car ride to where we were staying.

To this day I can't tell you what the scenery looked like. I only had eyes for marauding camels carrying blood-thirsty wailing Arabs. I must have realized real quick that my sneaky-but-lethal left hook wouldn't carry the day, because I remember getting my handkerchief ready. Upon attack, I was going to wave it out the window, while yelling at the top of my lungs, "Just Actors! Just Actors!!"

Fortunately my heads-up thinking wasn't needed. We arrived without incident. It was at that moment, my hankie came into use. Wiping some sweat from my brow, I was heard to say, "Boy, is it hot out here!" That was true in more ways than one.

On many locations, we were doing scenes with

machine guns trained on us from forty yards away. We had been warned by the production manager not to wander off even ten yards, or the gunners had a legit right to shoot us down. On these particular locations, I don't remember a single actor ever forgetting one line. Mental clarity was critical. Shoot. Print. Get the hell out of there. This certainly wasn't 'wonderful Copenhagen' anymore. Even *Inch Worm* was starting to have a certain appeal.

On the personal side, compared to Danny Kaye, my relationship with Kirk Douglas was strictly a healthy affair. Every morning he would ply me with fifteen vitamin pills. Up till then I'd never had a vitamin and this felt like overload. I balked somewhat, but he insisted. Maybe I was filling in for his sons, because it felt that fatherly.

There was only one no-no for Kirk. Don't out-juggle him, which I had a tendency to do. Not cool because he was playing a world-renowned juggler, teaching me to juggle. Unlike Danny Kaye, this had nothing to do with competition. The fact was when I was taught to juggle for the film, I loved it. Practiced all the time and became better than Kirk. No surprise. What else did I have to do, where as Kirk had a world of commitments on a variety of issues. There was always someone needing to see him for one thing or another. Being a movie star was a full time job.

When I had a day off, all I did was wonder why I hadn't received a letter from the girl back home in over a month. I refused to believe love was on the wane. Preferring to think she had a serious flu, I was certain letters would be pouring in any day. As I was picturing her face buried in my chest, glancing up adoringly while on a picturesque horse and buggy ride through Central Park, I was informed that a young girl by the name of Yael Dayan had come by to see me.

Yael was the daughter of a very famous commander in the Israeli military by the name of Moshe Dayan, a very charismatic guy who'd lost an eye during a battle and wore a black patch, making him look as dramatic a warrior as one can get. Yael, a pretty bold personality herself, had come by army jeep to take me swimming. No nonsense about her, just let's go. I was close to being burned out with constant juggling, and with no love letters to read and reread, it didn't take much urging. Although I did have one problem. I was less than average as a swimmer, so the thought of drowning crossed my mind. As I say that, I realize the line above should have read…'much less than average'. Put another way, no Olympic committee worth their salt would be issuing me a swimsuit any time soon.

On my way to the Sea of Galilee, I was getting nervous enough to wish for a flat tire, because my mind was already viewing it as the 'fatal swim'. No such luck. When we arrived at the water, it looked deep, long, and foreboding. Yael, not realizing my life would be coming to an end real soon, joyfully pointed to a boat moored off shore and said, "Let's swim to the boat."

Distance can be deceiving on open water, but it looked like I could possibly make it, so off we went. What looked like a 100-yard swim to me turned out to be 500 yards! When I saw Yael reach the empty boat and climb on, I still had about 350 yards to go and was gassed. I'm pretty sure Yael now knew she didn't have Michael Phelps as a swimming partner. I really should have turned back no matter how bad it looked, because this really did feel like life and death. Even if I did make it to the boat, how was I ever going to make it back without a full days rest—or a ride by a friendly Dolphin.

It finally came down to…if you drown you drown. You can't feel sorry for yourself in the middle of the Sea of Galilee. When I finally reached the boat I was in full exhaustion. Having the strength to lift myself up was nowhere to be found, so being hoisted out of the water may not have looked too manly, but it was that or sinking.

After no longer than a five minute rest, she said, "Lets swim back." I did. When they write a book about heroes I hope I'm mentioned.

In a land riddled with complexity, our brief relationship felt like a breezy summer movie where two teenagers meet, develop a small crush, while fully aware it will be over by summer's end. Throughout the years, I kept track of Yael. She became a politician, author, and prominent member of the Knesset. Didn't surprise me at all. I knew her strength and adored her as well.

Ambushed at the Palace

After completing *The Juggler,* it was a right time to get back to New York. *Hans Christian Andersen* was due to open, and the advanced word on the picture was glowing. I could already see the reviews. Hometown kid makes good! Possibly great! Bring on the accolades! Unfortunately Bosley Crowther, the top movie critic of The New York Times, felt differently than the rest of the country. He called the movie 'lumpish'. I could have lived with that until he wrote—'and the less I say about Farley Granger and Joey Walsh is better for health and digestion.' Jesus! How could he hit a young kid with such a low blow?! Didn't he know I had a girlfriend who had dumped me a month earlier for a non-working actor, who had nothing but time on his hands? Talk of piling on.

Anyway, at least Sam Goldwyn was happy. *Andersen* turned out to be a critical and financial success. As for me, I was awarded a Gold Star for being named the best child actor in New York, followed by winning "Film Daily's Famous Five" award of 1953 for outstanding screen performance and professional achievement. Take that Mr. Bosley Crowther.

At age fifteen, Lee Strasberg and company invited me to join the world renowned Actors Studio, which would have made me the youngest member of the group. My father was flying high because he was pretty impressed by the Studio, and knew many of the actors that were a part of it. While working as a Sightseeing Guide on 46th and Broadway, Dad would buy the out-of-work Studio actors a sandwich whenever they would stop by. These particular actors certainly had a 'method' for acquiring a free meal, but they also knew it came with a price. Before the big gobble, they had to endure stories about me and my latest accomplishments.

It certainly took a toll on Dad's productivity as a tour guide, because I never once saw him sell a sightseeing ticket. Word on the street was, great guy but worst guide in the touring business. Lucky for Dad, his partner was the absolute best! Ralph was a hawk when it came to swooping down on tourists. Poor out-of-towners could be shopping for socks, but if they came anywhere near Ralph, they would soon find themselves on a tour bus heading for Chinatown.

I once asked my father if he ever toyed with the idea that Ralph hated splitting the take with him day after day, since Ralph was THE guy in their partnership.

Dad responded, "Who gives a shit what he hates, because THIS corner, which is MY corner, is the BEST corner in the whole, rotten, fucking business. So the bastard should thank his lucky stars I ever agreed to take him on in the first fucking place."

Besides having a way with words, my father had one small point going for him. The corner of 46th and Broadway is where the tour buses made their departure, making it Primo Real Estate. Sorry Ralph, my mom and I felt your pain and would like to thank you for keeping the Walsh family afloat throughout the years.

As far as me joining the Actors Studio, my manager was dead set against it; said it would destroy my naturalness. So I became the deciding vote. Since I didn't care about acting, and I was acting in everything, now they wanted me to go to school to act some more?? Somebody must have had me confused with a real 'ac-tor'. I was wholeheartedly on my manager's side. Certainly not because he was any great shakes as an acting coach. His main contribution to me was never say the same word at the same volume. Example being, "Help. HELP. Run, RUN". That was the extent of it, and it was good enough for me.

Not so much for dad, who was already worried that the William Morris Agency may have been right. They had urged me to relocate to Hollywood immediately following *The Juggler.* 'Strike while the iron is hot' was their thinking. With two big Hollywood movies under my belt, they could set up daily meetings for me with all the top producers and movie executives in town. Said I was a cinch to never be out of work. I would be doing movie after movie. Wrong thing to say to me. Leave my home and friends just so they could work me to death? Forget it. I was adamantly opposed.

My manager was on my side in this, but mostly for his own reasons. He also didn't want to leave New York, and felt threatened that the William Morris Agency would become all powerful in my life, and there would be no need for him. It was my firm belief that if Hollywood wanted me bad enough, they would call and fly me out to do a movie. That never happened and William Morris quickly lost interest in pursuing my career.

No sweat for me. New York hadn't lost interest. I was doing more TV than ever, when I received a telegram from Danny Kaye a year later, inviting my mother and me to see his one man show at New York's world famous Palace Theater. Judy Garland had recently thrilled them. Now it was Danny's turn. I was happy and surprised that Danny just viewed our previous eight month competition on *Andersen* as just fun and games. I knew it was for me, but I was never sure about Danny before the telegram. This was really a big deal to be invited to something like this.

It became more of a surprise when at the beginning of Danny's show, he started talking about *Hans Christian Andersen* and called for me to stand up. I hesitated, suddenly feeling a little shy. But Danny insisted, so I stood. Then he insisted I come up on stage. This was too much. My legs wouldn't move, but with the audience applauding in delight and Danny's insistence, I somehow managed to do it.

Soon as I climbed up on stage, Danny put his arm around my shoulder, turned to his orchestra leader as if planned and just said, "Maestro". With that, the orchestra started playing, 'Wonderful, Wonderful Copenhagen', whereupon Danny immediately encouraged me to sing along with him. There was nothing to do but comply. I started singing with him, but after a very short time Danny suddenly stopped and said to the audience, "Just as I remember. This kid has the worst singing voice, bar none."

The audience roared with amusement, Danny burst into laughter, and I managed a weak chuckle. Was Danny still in competitor mode...who knows? In truth, I was never much of a singer, but bar none?? Danny was lucky he never got caught in a dark alley with my mother.

Bruised but undaunted at being ambushed at the Palace, I trouped on, starring in numerous TV shows.

One in particular comes to mind because of the actor who played my older brother. A nice, shy midwestern kid with bad eye sight. We bet a dollar who was blinder of the two, and he won going away. Poor guy. I couldn't see shit without my glasses and he was worse. Off camera, he wore thick, tortoise shell glasses. Told me his poor vision was actually an advantage to him as an actor, because the theatrical lights made his eyes water, making him appear ultra sensitive.

For any person, sensitive or not, the show was a horror for him. Not all his fault, but grim and strangely comical at the same time. I believe the series was called 'Crime Syndicate', directed by a man named John Peyser. The plot was kind of a *West Side Story*. I was the leader of a street gang, trying to talk my older brother (played by this kid) back into the gang for an upcoming rumble.

As the camera moved past me into a big close-up for his lengthy answer, a gang member, who had ONE LINE in the show—forgot it—and said nothing. The dead silence screamed for rescue, so the actor playing my older brother jumped in to fill the dreaded empty space. What ensued was a fiasco. He got tongue-twisted so badly that everything he said was nonsensical. Painful to watch. So Daffy Duck-ish in fact, it created a nervous energy in me that seriously threatened to go out of control.

Lucky the camera was on him and not me, because I was literally fighting my whole body to not break out in full laughter—a monumental struggle of face contorting and mouth squeezing. It was that horrifying to watch. This was why actors feared live television. In one split second your career could be finished. What a terrible way to go out. Because of another actor missing his cue, he had destroyed himself. I felt bad that this would probably be the last time show business would ever see the sensitive, shy, blind kid from the midwest—His name was James Dean.

Let Him Eat His Pork Chops in Peace

For some young boys, their first shave was something to be proud of. But for yours truly, it spelled trouble. It seemed like I was suddenly too old to play the kid anymore and too young to play the adult. The dreaded in-between age had arrived. The Random House Dictionary describes 'has-been' as a person or thing that is no longer effective, successful, or popular. Certainly my status as being THE biggest child star in New York had seen better days. I wasn't in Walter Winchell or Jack O'Brian's daily column as much as I used to be, that's for sure. There was plenty of love for a ten to fifteen year old juvenile delinquent, but for a sixteen year old with a hint of peach fuzz, not so much.

Yet I still had enough name value to do a big press conference showcasing Floyd Patterson. He was about to fight for the heavyweight championship, and they wrote a comic parody for me to do. It was called 'Why was I born?' Everybody got a big kick out of it. Even painfully shy Floyd, who managed to lift his head and crack a smile.

Floyd said very little, but when asked some random question, remarked in a tiny voice, "It's easy to do anything in victory. It's in defeat that a man reveals himself." Heady stuff for someone who was soon to become the youngest heavyweight champion in history. All I could think was, lucky him. What I would have given to trade places. The dream of fighting for a world title had never left me.

While my father had prevailed in stopping me from becoming a professional fighter, it never stopped him from taking me to many of the big fights. If I couldn't be in the ring myself, being at the fights was still the second best thing. My night at Yankee Stadium to see Rocky Marciano fight Archie Moore for the heavyweight title was pretty exciting stuff, but what happened after the fight was even more thrilling.

My father was an expert at making quick exits after a big fight or you'd have an hour wait or longer to catch a ride. Sure enough, we caught the last cab in sight. As we started to pull away, there was urgent knocking on my window. It was Sugar Ray Robinson! The greatest fighter for me, then and now, was asking if we could give him a lift to his famous restaurant & bar, Sugar Rays. It was a pretty short trip from Yankee Stadium, but that didn't matter. He could have been asking to go to the moon and back for all I cared. This was SUGAR RAY ROBINSON! I couldn't believe it!!

As much as this was a trip for me, it turned out to be an eye-opener for the Sugar man. He had just run into a young white boy, who not only idolized him, but knew his entire fight record by memory. At that point, his record stood at 136 wins. 88 knockouts, 4 losses, 2 draws. Also I could name most of his opponents, and that really blew him away! On top of all that, here was a kid, sincerely telling him I feared for his safety in his upcoming title fight against Carl 'Bobo' Olson. My concern started years earlier when I saw him at Roosevelt Stadium in Jersey City. Light-hitting Charlie Fusari went fifteen rounds with him. By NOT knocking out Fusari, I was scared that Sugar had 'lost a step'.

My father jumped in to save Sugar from his kid's earnestness: "Sugar carried Fusari that night."

Sugar tried to relieve my angst by saying, "I might have been a bit gentle on the young man that evening."

I sure hoped so, because Sugar retired soon after that night, and here he was back three years later to take on Bobo Olson, who was on a torrid run, destroying all the middleweight contenders in his path. I had watched Sugar's two comeback fights in preparation for Olson, and it didn't relieve my stress for Sugar's chances against Mr. Olson. Sugar had lost badly to Ralph Tiger Jones, and won a split decision against Rocky Castellani, a fight where he was dropped, and I thought he lost. Certainly these were worthy enough fighters, but nothing a younger Sugar couldn't have handled with ease.

After I unloaded all my concerns on him, Sugar put his arm around me and told me no need for worry. Said the fight was going to be a walk in the park and that he would knockout Olson within two rounds. He then wrote his phone number on a piece of paper and said to call him tomorrow; he'd make sure my father and I would be sitting ringside as his guests when he flattens Bobo—just for me. Also, he said with a wink, if he was a betting man, he'd be taking the 3 to 1 odds against him.

As high as I was that night, my father took the wind out of my sails when he later informed me he had no intention of calling for the tickets, because Sugar never said anything about paying for the air flight to Chicago Stadium. I pleaded with Dad to change his mind, but much to my distress, he held firm. Just couldn't afford it, he said, so stop begging.

I never knew the real story until mom clued me in years later. Dad was concerned if he called Sugar, most definitely he'd be offered all paid for fight AND flight tickets. That was Sugar Ray's style. First class all the way. This shook my father to the core, because what he didn't want to tell me was… he was deathly afraid of flying.

The only thing that came out of that crushing disappointment was the $480 I won when Sugar Ray knocked out Bobo Olson at 2:51 of the SECOND ROUND!

While that was my highlight of 1955, the low point came when Jimmy Dean was killed in a car crash on a California highway at age 24. Even though we only played make believe brothers on TV, it felt like a death in the family. I thought about his poor eyesight. Was he wearing his glasses? Did he, or did he not, see his doom coming? It was unreal. Here was a guy who was a REAL actor, got what he wanted, and this was the payoff?! Didn't seem right.

As far as my Dad was concerned, Dean's death was the perfect opportunity for one of his typical dinner rants. "See the shit that happens unless you take the bull by the horn and stab the bastard in the back". This was father speak for: GET A FUCKIN' HAIRCUT...QUIT SLEEPING SO FUCKIN' LATE...GET RID OF THAT DIRTY RAT BASTARD MANAGER...FIND NEW FUCKIN' REPRESENTATION, ETC.

Mom usually interrupted the verbal barrage at some point by telling him to knock off the curse words, and let me eat my pork chops in peace. Always a bad move on her part, because now she was under fire for coddling me, AND for the grease in the pork chops which always caused him heartburn.

Unquestionably, Dad was hurting big time with my fading career. When prestige television such as Playhouse 90, Studio One, Kraft Theatre, along with Hollywood, lost my phone number, it was more than he could handle. Standing on his corner, raving about his kid became a thing of the past. It didn't hurt my ego. My issue was strictly shortage of cash. This left the door open for a daytime soap opera to swoop in and cast me for a recurring role.

This was certainly a new experience. Instead of rehearsing for a week on premium television, this meant learning a full hour script every day. No problem for 'soap' pros, because they could see their lines on a teleprompter. All I could see was a blur of letters, so I was at a major disadvantage. The first three shows were basically miracles. I remembered all my lines. On the fourth show, my luck ran out.

I was in practically every scene in the show, and right from the start I went up. Couldn't remember a line. Had no clue who my character was, nor the point of the show. A total blank. Pretty terrifying. My heart rate was moving fast, but my tongue was moving faster. It was actually amazing how verbal I became. Words were spewing out with a nice sense of logic, but it had no relationship with the story line of that particular episode.

The poor girl working with me didn't stand a chance. She did a lot of nodding, and trying her best to respond to whatever the hell I was talking about. Each time I rushed off to the next set up, I tried to remember something—anything—of what the script was about.

Never happened. I just kept making crap up, so that the TV audience wouldn't notice anything was wrong. Never once was I at a loss for words. And the stuff that was coming out felt pretty good. Much better than the junk I was supposed to say. A future writer? Nah, never gave it a thought.

After the show ended, it was routine for the director's voice to come over the sound system to thank the cast and crew, which he did, while adding, "But I don't know how to thank Joey Walsh for that entire new show, so lets leave it at that, shall we."

A few days went by before I got the 'word'. Next show I would die in a car crash. It wasn't subtle how they felt about me, but it also didn't compute because I had been given another play date after that. When I questioned, there must be some mistake, they cleared it up real fast. I would come back as a ghost. No dialogue required.

Now a normal person might be upset where things were at, but not me. Jimmy Dean had lost his life in a car crash, I just lost a soap. Big deal. This cavalier attitude of mine drove my father even crazier than before. How come I wasn't as miserably depressed as he was about my career situation?! Was I just too stupid to see the handwriting on the wall, which spelled out 'LOSER'.

What my father didn't know was that I DID see the handwriting on the wall. And what it spelled out to me was the word WINNER! My hidden confidence was based on the belief that I was the greatest college football handicapper known to man. I was especially uncanny at predicting the spread winners in the Ivy League. I just seemed to know when Harvard would knock off Yale, Brown would upset Columbia, Penn would beat Dartmouth, etc. When it came to intelligent guy, beating intelligent guy, I knew better then all the smart-money guys. All I had to do was find a bookmaker (BM) who would take my action and the rest would be history. A handicapping legend would be born. I was more excited about this prospect than winning any Oscar.

Louie the Bookie

When I first met Louie the bookmaker in his little Italian grocery store, my heart was beating fast. His Doberman Pinscher was inches away from my manhood and growling menacingly. I thought my sex life was about to experience the same fate as my acting career, when Louie simply said, "Irene, go back and powder your nose." The Doberman left.

"Nice trained poodle you got there," I said, barely breathing. I don't know what possessed me to say something that lame, but can only attribute it to trying to sound cool and hide my case of the shakes.

He studied me momentarily. "So I hear you're looking for some action."

"You hears good." Swear to god I don't know who was feeding me this dialogue, but prayed it would dry up fast before I blew the whole deal. Fortunately, it didn't seem to faze Louie as he said with a notable air of confidence, "Well kid, you've come to the right place. Everybody beats me like a drum."

Despite being handed a snow job, my mind kept thinking—I don't know about 'everybody', but I knew SOMEONE who was destined to give you a big headache. My headache had come a few days earlier when I approached my father on the touchy subject of retrieving my life's earnings. Surprisingly, he was very easy about it.

"You want your money, you got it. All $91 of it."

At first I hoped it was a joke, but something about the one dollar part of the ninety was too exacting for my comfort. When he proceeded to rattle on about the cost of school tuition, food, clothing, prescription glasses, I knew I was in big trouble. Later, I learned that my less-than-inspiring-nest-egg was due to Dad's hapless handicapping in the stock market, plus his personal weakness of losing my money betting on Harness racing. Nonetheless, I still had Louie, so why worry about money. I would be a zillionaire in no time.

So with my measly $91 tucked in my pocket, I was on the hunt to secure a few dollars more, which led me straight to a close friend from Professional Children School days. Displaying great salesmanship, I gushed over my newly acquired bank vault—namely Louie. Still, it was difficult for Elliott Gould (yes, that Elliott Gould) to invest his only $60 in the world on my ingenious plan. It seems it had taken him months of saving his small weekly allowance, along with some rotten little after school job to accumulate this sum. He was uttering some nonsense about it being lunch money for the month, plus his tap dance lesson money. I couldn't buy any of it, and since Elliott always had a problem with saying 'no', I got his entire sixty bucks. Our dough combined gave me all I needed to put my sure-fire scheme into operation.

The plan was simple: Go down to the Italian grocery store, plunk down the whole wad on my fifteen super duper football picks, then come back later to collect our winnings. The only blip came on a 'pick'em' game. With our team leading 14-0, the other team came up with fourteen points in the last quarter to tie us, creating no winner either way. The other fourteen games breezed home just like a sound plan should. Elliott looked at me like I was some freak of nature. I'll never forget the pride I felt when Louie handed back my winning slip and said, "Take this fucking thing and frame it." I, on the other hand, was still miffed about that ONE game ending in a tie. Felt like I was robbed.

Fourteen wins and a push. Not a bad start on the way to riches beyond belief. I felt invincible. As unbelievable as it sounds, we bet on every sport, including hockey, over the next few months, and never had one single losing day!

Talking Dirty

Dizzy from the heights, and wearing our newly purchased Camel Hair coats, we flew off to humid 90 degree Miami for wine, women and a visit to see Elliott's father. Feeling like the hippest and 'coolest' customers in town (forget the coats), we headed to the world famous Fontainebleau hotel one night. Headlining the showgirls was Sandi, the most beautiful girl on the planet— AND WE KNEW HER! She had gone to Professional Children's School with us. Only Elliott and I had never spoken one word to her. As far as we could remember nobody did, because when she walked by, every guy's mouth just hung open, unable to do anything but drool.

By the end of the evening Elliott headed out to see his father, and I decided to take a gamble. I gave the Maitre d' twenty bucks to deliver a note. It read, 'Hi Sandi, do you remember me from Mrs. Levy's French class?' It must have carried a huge sexual undertone because I hit pay dirt. After five blissful days, the somewhat skinnier, little dead-end kid from New York made a fatal mistake.

Being fairly new at the sex stuff, and not into bad language, I was taken off guard when the 'creature' asked me to talk dirty to her. I tried to let it slide, but the pressure was on when she kept insisting. There was no way to duck this one.

Mustering all the courage I could, while desperately trying to recall some of my father's foul dialogue, I gave her one more mighty thrust, simultaneously yelling, "Take that, you dirty rat bastard!"

The silence that filled that room was downright eerie. I thought immediately of going limp and faking an appendicitis attack, but it seemed just too cowardly. Hopefully my previous performances would carry the day. Upon leaving I told her I'd give her a call, and she said not to bother because her phone was out of order. 'Dirty rat bastard' may have worked for James Cagney and Dad, but it was surely the kiss of death for me.

Desperate Boys Do Desperate Things

After the big sizzle fizzled, I went straight to the dogs. After three weeks of never finding a Greyhound racer even mildly interested in the rabbit, Elliott and I were tapped out. The glorious hot streak had ended, not with a bang, but a whimper. I don't know how it felt to Elliott, but to me it just called for a little creative thinking—as in, call up Louie, explain where I was, and make bets over the phone. Undoubtedly, we'd be flush again by next week. Losing was never an option in my mind.

Much to my stunned disbelief, the unthinkable happened. We were swept! I bet eight games and lost them all. My dreams of being the 'pig-skin' prophet were badly diminished, but still more serious was the fact that I owed $880 to a bookmaker I had beaten for $25,000, without ever paying him once! Worse yet, there was no way to come up with that kind of money. Impossible.

Fleetingly, I thought of never returning home again, but being on the lam for the rest of my life seemed too drastic. Instead, I decided to go back, face up to the bookie, explain my dog misadventures, and claim I was just a mixed up kid who had lost his way. With my acting experience, and memory of Skippy the dead dog, I managed to extract a tear and it worked like a charm.

He accepted the story and my promise to pay ten dollars a week until the debt was paid. I was never so thrilled in my life. Facing sure death, I was off the hook, except for TEN DOLLARS A WEEK! It was too good to be true. I remember babbling to him that there wasn't a more understanding human being on the face of the earth, and that I didn't deserve to be standing in the presence of such a great man. He told me to knock off the bullshit and just make sure I never miss a payment. I swore up and down that I would never fail him again, and genuinely meant every word.

I made one ten dollar payment, then missed the next two. It seemed like every dollar I got my hands on, which wasn't much, was needed to be in action. Bad thinking.

In the middle of a moonlit night, I woke to an ominous figure standing near the entrance of my bedroom. My luck had run out. I was frozen. How did he get past my parent's bedroom? Oh god, what did he do to them?! Why was he just standing there? Silent torture. I couldn't make out his face, but his hoodlum Fedora and top coat spelled trouble. I know my offense was kinda serious, but never to this degree. I couldn't speak. Just stared, waiting for him to make his move. It took forever for me to realize it was ME standing there.

I had been drinking that night and when I got home, put my wise guy hat and topcoat over the upright ironing board before crashing into sleep. Talk about foreshadowing.

The very next night, when Louie showed up at my apartment with rage in his eyes and murder in his heart, is something I will never forget. At the very least I knew my legs were sure goners. Broken beyond repair. Yet by the time he left, they were still intact and I had a hundred dollars of his money in my pocket.

Here's how that came down: In our neighborhood, we lost our electricity every week or so for about five to fifteen minutes at a time. It was always considered a real pain in the ass as we then had to break out the candles. That evening it was particularly annoying because I was in the hurried process of polishing up the Gold Star awarded me, so I could get to the pawn shop before it closed. I needed the dough to bet on a fight that night.

So when the doorbell rang and I opened it to a homicidal ranting Louie, the house was dark and I was holding my little shiny Gold Star. With my father away at the Trotters, the commotion quickly brought Mom to the door, carrying a lit candle. I assured her that everything was okay (not that I believed it), and convinced her to leave us alone. Reluctantly, she did.

I immediately turned to the rabid Bookie and explained to the foam on his mouth how we were living in darkness because we had no money to pay our electricity bill. Told him I was just about to hock my beloved Gold Star to raise some money so my poor mother wouldn't have to go on living in blackness, with hot wax spilling over her hands. It was a desperate gamble because I knew the lights were about to come on any minute. But desperate boys do desperate things.

The bookmaker, like the Wicked Witch of the West, just seemed to melt on the spot. With moisture in his eyes, he reached into his pocket, then handed me a C-note, saying, "I love my family too." With that, he turned and headed down the stairs, JUST as the lights came on! In sheer panic, I violently slammed the door shut! I've often wondered what he thought of my fierce reaction to his generous gesture.

Anyway, I immediately went out and bet the hundred on a fighter I knew couldn't lose. He lost.

Going for Broke

Now you might think that after God spared me from having a Genoa salami strangled around my neck, I would reconsider my risky behavior. Not a chance. That's for people who had a head on their shoulders, not up their ass. That's why a few months later, after winning 200 bucks playing great table tennis (ping-pong), I found myself in a limo with two buddies, facing three goons who would give Luca Brasi of *Godfather* fame, a run for his money.

We were heading out of New York City into the wilds of New Jersey, where a floating crap game was being held. It took some coaxing from me to get my friends to put up fifty bucks apiece to attend this 'Guys and Dolls-like' event, and now felt they weren't too happy with me. Who could blame them? Sitting directly across from this threesome was enough to put shivers up your spine. They just stared at us. Never blinked.

I was doing my best to avoid eye contact, but every so often I would sneak a peek at the triplets from hell, which turned out to be one 'peek' too many. A serious case of the giggles followed. Couldn't stop. I was out of control. My friends knew what was happening, and were scared to death we'd be ice-picked on the spot.

I desperately tried to cover for my suicidal behavior by telling my buddies I couldn't stop laughing at all the hilarious things that happened to me when I was nine years old. I went on making up shit like that for what seemed like the longest car ride in history. I was acting like the most lighthearted idiot on the planet, but at least we were still alive when we arrived at the crap game.

As we entered a farmhouse in the black of night, we were confronted by two guys who immediately frisked us. I felt the giggles come on again, but managed to hold it in. Two of the Luca Brasi triplets, being old pros at this, handed over their revolvers, which were then hung on a wall next to eleven other guns. My friends and I were trying to appear calm, but our lives were flashing before us as we were led into a large area where the dice game was in progress.

There must have been seventy guys encircling a crap table, and off to the side, a man sitting on top a wooden stepladder. He was holding a Tommy gun. This was definitely no giggling matter. I whispered to my friends to stay cool and we'd be alright. I wasn't exactly buying it, but acted like I did, and waved casually to the man with the Tommy gun as we passed by on the way to the table.

As we approached, a sea of unfriendly eyes glanced our way, then thankfully dismissed us. The pressure we all felt was pretty intense, but got worse when it came my turn to shoot the dice. The house man would roll the dice across the table into each shooter's cupped hand, and then in one motion the shooter would roll the dice. I assumed it was being done this way so that nobody could slip in 'loaded' dice.

The only problem was, I couldn't catch the dice cleanly in my cupped hand. They would just bounce off my palm and the process would have to be repeated. Sometimes I would catch one, but never two. Well, this didn't set too well with the broken-nose crowd. Especially the ones who were 'stuck' at the moment. Also, the return of the giggles didn't help matters. Finally, I managed to catch the dice and proceeded to go on a very 'hot roll'. I was doing fabulous, but wasn't making any friends because the majority of the players were betting against me, and losing consistently.

I was so turned on by how well I was doing that I didn't notice the furtive glances being exchanged among the players. Fortunately or unfortunately, my friends did, and whispered to me if I kept winning, we'd never get out of there alive. They quietly begged me to lose the money back and leave fast. I hated the idea. But they were so convinced I would get them killed, I agreed to keep doubling up every bet until I lost. Well, I couldn't lose. I made pass after pass, with the whole joint growing ever more hostile. Even my friends started to groan in upset with every winning roll, making me the only villain in the place. I wasn't doing it on purpose. What did they want from me? It was bad enough I couldn't enjoy a most incredible run, but when I started to get secretly ankle-kicked by my friends for each WINNING roll it was difficult to take.

Finally I made everybody's dream come true except for mine. When I 'seven-ed' out a cheer erupted, which included my buddies, and I was left feeling miserable. Thousands of winning dollars gone in an instant and all I had left to show for it was a rotten twelve dollar profit. As we were leaving, there was a guy taking action on the Number for the next day, which worked like this: However much was wagered at the racetrack that day, was posted in the paper later that night. The last three numbers of the total handle would be the winning numbers. It was a thousand to one shot that paid 600 to 1 if you hit. Most people at the time bet two or three dollars. Since I wanted to get rid of any reminder of what just happened to me I bet the whole twelve on 556, because those were the numbers I hit the most on my hot dice run.

The next day, 556 hit. The first time I ever played a number, I hit it for twelve bucks! $7200!!! I was ecstatic, until my friends told me no thug in his right mind is going to pay a couple of kids $7200 for a twelve dollar bet! Then added if I went out to collect, they wouldn't be going with, because they were sure to end up buried somewhere in a New Jersey farm field. Since I'd never gotten over deliberately losing all the money back the night before, I refused to listen. I believed it was worth taking a chance to get killed for $7200. They wholeheartedly didn't agree, and said if I went out there alone, they would accept just a grand apiece, and that I could keep the other $5200!

Well that just sweetened the pot so much I was ready to go—until news came in that the crap game had been raided and scores of people arrested. I was crushed. How could this happen to me?! I had the hottest run of my life in dice, hit the number 556, and all I had to show for it was an extreme case of nausea. My world was getting crazier by the minute.

Excuse Me, Mr. Sinatra

Not long after the crap game tragedy, I was too busy being young and foolish to realize more trouble would soon be heading my way. I had discovered Jilly's Bar. It was located on 52nd Street, west of Broadway, and was the place to be. Terrific singer-piano player. Great looking girls. Loved it. Best of all, the owner, Jilly Rizzo, took a real liking to me, and upon finding out my dire financial situation, let me run a tab. He even sent drinks over to some girls and said it came from me.

"Pay me when your ship comes in, kid," he would always say.

You had to like this guy. I know Frank Sinatra must've felt the same way because he and Jilly became life long friends. In fact, I was there the night Sinatra walked in with two men and was introduced to Jilly. The thing that got to me that evening was the BLACK BRIEFCASE. It was carried by one of Sinatra's guys, and every time Sinatra made a motion it was given to him and immediately snapped open.

What a sight! Rows and rows of neatly stacked $100 bills, which Sinatra generously gave to the help. Two hundred a piece for the cocktail waitresses, and hundreds more for the Maitre d', piano player, bouncer, bus boy, etc. All in all, he must have handed out at least $1200 in tips.

Since I was sitting so close to him, my mind churned in every direction. Maybe he would look over, nod wryly, snap open the brief case and hand me a couple hundred, saying, "Here, kid, you look like you're desperate to bet a three team football parlay." Nah. I like long shots but that was a little too far out even for me. Better yet, why don't I just say, "Excuse me, Mr. Sinatra, I don't know if you remember me, but I worked with you on the Frank Sinatra TV show. Played Ben Blue's son in the weekly comedy sketch."

My hesitation with that approach was twofold: It had been five years. AND back then Sinatra was at the lowest ebb of his career. Besides not singing very well, his show was competing with The Milton Berle Hour. A total mismatch because no one missed Uncle Milty's hour, including my parents. Sinatra didn't even have a sponsor for the first eleven weeks, until the Bulova Watch Company opened their wallet for the last two Christmas shows.

During that time, Sinatra never seemed to be in a happy mood, and anything could set him off. Long rehearsal hours in a darkened theater, tended to make people nod off. Sinatra, either paranoid or whatever, would claim there was too much whispering, and abruptly leave the stage. He was definitely in a bad way, and when the news came that the show was being canceled, moods got worse.

Since it wasn't a fun show I didn't much care about the cancellation, but kinda felt bad for Mr. Sinatra. Because of that I decided to buy him a necktie as a going away present. Even though he seldom spoke to me, he smiled when I gave him the tie. It was a striking moment, realizing I'd never seen him smile in all the weeks I worked on his show.

He looked at me for a long beat.. "Thanks, kid. Good luck with your career. You're good," then turned and walked away.

His communication landed. There's something about honesty that goes straight for where it counts and makes a difference.

When the final show ended, everybody milled around saying their goodbyes, but when I looked for Sinatra he wasn't there. So I headed back to his dressing room, not only for the final farewell, but also in hopes of getting one more glimpse of the stunningly beautiful Ava Gardner, who often came to pick him up after shows. Unfortunately, neither were there.

His door was wide open, and the dressing room bare of everything, except for a clothes rack in the center of the room—where only my tie had been conspicuously left behind. It stopped me momentarily, but it hardly mattered that he didn't like my taste in ties. Earlier, in a span of less than 20 seconds, he'd gotten across how he felt about me, so leaving my tie behind would be far from a life-scarring event. In all honesty, missing one more sighting of the jaw-dropping Ava, was a little tougher to take.

These were the memories I was sitting with when trying to get my mind in a place where it could extract a few stray C-notes from Mr. Sinatra. He had recently won the Academy award for his performance in the movie *From Here To Eternity*, so he was flying high and his spirit and generosity were showing it. Like a geyser, he was spewing out hundreds to those a little less fortunate. I considered myself in worse shape than the help, so why shouldn't I be part of the 'big giveaway'. But looking like a conniver with a sad sack story wasn't coming forth. Integrity was getting the best of me. Shit, where was my backbone when I needed it.

"Don't Bull Me, Mister"

Being able to run a tab at Jilly's worked well for my social life, but also created an awkward moment one night. A very stunning girl came by my table and thanked me for her drink. I was somewhat surprised but didn't show it, because I knew right away this had to be Jilly's doing. A bigger surprise came when she asked if she could join me for the drink. Since I was feeling somewhat down, mulling over my financial woes and no job offers, this came as a nice lift.

We hit it off great, and the more we drank, the stronger the connection grew. I remember being naturally amusing and we laughed a lot. Felt like I didn't have a care in the world—until she said enthusiastically, "I'm starving. Would you like to take me for bacon and eggs? "

Usually when a guy is hit with a line like that, it's a big yes, yes, moment. Only for me, it was 'oh shit, no.'

She immediately picked up my slight hesitation. "Aren't you hungry?"

Actually, I was starving as well, but my mind was racing to my pocket, trying to mentally count out if I had enough dough to cover breakfast. I knew it was going to be a close call. Maybe if I just had a cup of coffee and she didn't order anything more than bacon and eggs, I could squeeze by. God forbid the 'big spender' would be exposed as having only six dollars and change in his entire bankroll.

While caught up in this life drama, the cocktail waitress came by to tell me there were a few men at the back table that wanted to see me. When I questioned the situation, she said, "I think you better talk to them." While not in the mood for whatever this was, something in her tone told me I better go back there. At least it would give me a little more time to think out my breakfast dilemma.

As I approached some very unfriendly faces, I gathered up my best tough-guy demeanor. "I was told you wanted to see me."

"Is this the kid?" the head man said, staring at me with fire in his eyes.

"That's him," came a solemn voice.

"You beat our office for fifty thousand fucking dollars, then stiffed us for $880?!"

It was actually down to 870, but saying I'd coughed up 10 bucks was not the way to handle this. Despite the guy's real-sounding threat, I kept up my best strongman front, saying I didn't know who he was, which was in fact true. He told me he was the Italian grocery store, and everything in me wanted to say, that's funny, you don't look like the Italian grocery store. Thankfully, I managed to keep a clamp on that reply.

"First of all, I didn't win $50,000; it was 25. And that's all being taken care of with Louie, who runs the store," I said.

With that, the head man reached out and yanked on my tie, pulling me toward him. His sinister voice wasn't playacting when he said, "It better be taken care of."

I pulled back and countered with, "Don't bull me, mister. I don't take that stuff from nobody."

This by the way, is very bad conversation to use with these type of guys, but yanking my tie like that, felt really out of line. Besides, my upgrade in ties had come a long way since the one I foisted on Sinatra, so that also helped in pissing me off.

When I got back to my table, the stunning girl must have noticed my stern expression.

"What's wrong?" she said.

This was a big moment for me. I could use it to own up to the fact that I wasn't any big shot made of money. I knew that truth was powerful, and could work in my favor...but I wasn't up to it. Too much pressure for one evening. So I said in my best cool guy fashion, "Breaking my heart to leave you, but something's come up that I can't talk about. Catch up with you later, beautiful."

Better to leave looking like a man of mystery, rather than hear her say the dreaded words—'extra bacon'.

Roy's Bowling Alley

Three weeks later, I found out the 'tie yanker' wasn't kidding around. Two rather large men, claiming to be detectives, showed up at my apartment. They were asking my mother if I was home just as I entered the room. Without hesitation they rushed me. Somehow Mom managed to stay between me and them, yelling to leave her son alone. They were definitely there to do damage to my body, but with Mom screaming and pushing at them, they stopped.

After a long tense beat, they settled for telling her, "Your son has been a naughty boy and if he doesn't shape up, which means pay up, he's gonna get a real good spanking!" With that, they turned and left.

At the time, I'm sure I didn't give it the weight it deserved, but suspected I should pay off the Italian grocery store because they were being no fun about the whole thing. Of course, the way my brain operated at the time, the only way to do that was to gamble and win.

This led to a place that anybody in their right mind could tell was trouble. It should have been posted with warning signs:

ENTER AT YOUR OWN RISK—
PROCEED WITH CAUTION—
TURN AND RUN AS FAST AS YOU CAN

Roy's Bowling Alley was a place so ominous that it could have been the model for the barroom scene in the first *Star Wars*. Full with creatures-of-the-night in all frightening shapes and sizes. Thieves, muggers, killers and everything in between, would gather there to gamble big time at Barrel Pins. It was played on a regular size bowling alley, but instead of using regulation size, or duckpins, they used the much smaller barrel pin and a smaller ball, minus finger holes. If you scored in the mid to high nineties, you were quite a player.

Somehow, I turned out to be a natural at this game. I would waltz in around 2 AM looking like a young Leonardo DiCaprio wearing my one silk suit and exaggerated rolled collar. This was meant to convey deep pockets. If I wasn't a tender looking morsel to be devoured by these denizens of the deep, I don't know who was. They were salivating over who would get first bite out of me.

As a successful child actor, turned has-been, I knew my way around drama, and played my role to the hilt. I acted as if I could lose a fortune, and what could I win from them?! Unless they made me an offer I couldn't refuse, I wouldn't be losing my wad to anybody! After all, I had thousands to lose, maybe millions. Why shouldn't I get the best of the handicap!! I believed my performance so much, that not only did it make perfect sense to me, I convinced them as well. I made the pot of gold so alluring and so available to be plundered, that they were falling over each other trying to please me with the best of it.

Luckily, they never found out how little they were chasing, because I never lost. Night after night, I would win a few hundred bucks without working up a sweat. I sure wasn't making a lot of friends raking in the dough, but I could live with that. At least that's what I thought—until things got a little dicey.

One night, a well-dressed man in his early forties walked in and was immediately swarmed by the unholy inhabitants. I can't recall his name, but 'Mark' should suffice, because that's how he was treated as everyone clamored to bowl him. This was a guy who came in about every six months, looking to roll barrel pins and lose a few grand to whoever was lucky enough to play him. Not knowing any of this history at the time, I was unprepared for what happened next.

While everybody was hawking themself as an opponent, Mark literally pushed his way through the ghoulish throng and came over to me.

84

"Don't I know you?"

Turns out he knew my face from television, and when that fact was established, he was really impressed. Asked if I wanted a little action bowling him. At first I said no, because I didn't know how good he was. Lefty, the pin boy, and the only guy who liked me in the place, quietly told me Mark's story. Then urged me to bowl him because I couldn't lose.

Lefty was right. I beat the guy easily for eighteen hundred dollars! Graciously, he thanked me for playing him and left good-naturedly. What an easy score. Too easy. While I was being thrilled, and thrilling Lefty with a two hundred dollar tip, my good spirits were quickly dashed. Whitey from Flushing (as he was known) came up to me and said he wanted half my win, because I stole his game.

Since everybody knew the truth of what happened, including Whitey, this was strictly a strong-arm play that I wasn't buying. Right from the start when I first came to Roy's, I was told to stay clear of Whitey. He was real bad news. A mugger by trade who was never satisfied unless he heard something crack on the body. On top of that, it was obvious this slime always hated me with a passion and was just itching for an excuse to hurt me. So when he informed me he would break both my arms and legs if he didn't get half the dough, it was undoubtedly true.

A buddy, who happened to be with me that night, knew I was in deep shit and said he wanted to call his father. I didn't like this for two reasons: Being a kid who always fought his own battles, I hated the thought of someone's father being called to protect me; AND I thought it would just make matters worse. I mean, c'mon, why would this animal listen to anybody's father on the phone?? This wasn't grade school.

Yet, my buddy convinced me that despite my sneaky-but-lethal-left hook, I didn't stand a chance against this guy's strength, size and awesome reputation. At least his father might have the type of clout needed for a grim situation. After all, my buddy's father wasn't in the law-abiding business himself, even though we never knew exactly what he did. What we did know was that we once walked into the Red Devil Restaurant, just off 48th and Broadway, and saw him having dinner with the two biggest names in organized crime at the time — Albert Anastasia and Frank Costello! I remember my buddy's father proudly saying that I played tough delinquent kids on television, and that really pleased them. Anastasia actually patted my arm and told me to keep up the good work. And he meant it.

At any rate, I let my buddy call his father because, as he stated, he won't be home anyway. That kind of logic won me over. As it turned out, he was home, and having dinner with a friend named Pittsburgh Phil. After hearing the story, he said to stay by the phone. He'd call back in two minutes. He called back in one, "Tell Whitey from Flushing there's a phone call for him."

Later, we heard that Pittsburgh Phil's conversation with Whitey had these kind of elements attached to it:

Cut off nuts that would be stuffed in mouth. A dick cut in two that would be rammed into the ears, and a scorched torso that would be hung from the largest pole in Flushing. To avoid this, Whitey was to become instantly religious and start praying that no ill fell upon me, now or ever. Even a bad flu might be held against him and trigger all his fingers being cut off and shoved up his nose.

Nice wholesome conversation. But it obviously worked because after the phone call, Whitey from Flushing left the bowling alley immediately, never to return. I should have been as smart as Whitey, but this dregs of a place became my obsessional hangout, gambling at barrel pins all night long.

Of course, coming home every morning around eleven and sleeping till dinner time became problematic for Dad. Arguments never stopped. He was locked into his position, and I didn't like being locked in, so it went nowhere. My mom always told me it was senseless battling with him because he wasn't going to change. One day when he was hell-bent on finding out 'what the fuck' I was doing to all hours of the morning, I decided to spare Mom the headache of listening to us flail away at each other, and simply said: "I was having an appointment with adventure." Why anything such as that came out of my mouth, I have no idea, but knew it was time to quickly leave the dinner table.

I expected him to erupt any moment, but a strange silence ensued. It was bewildering. Total quiet in a situation such as this, wasn't my father. I crept back to a spot to where I could listen and not be seen.

As the eerie silence dragged on, I wondered if I had discovered some secret formula on how to deal with dad that would spare the family a lot of grief. I was straining to hear something, anything, and then I heard…

"This is your fault, Kitty."

"Don't start," she countered.

"Don't you care about anything that's going on with that idiot son of yours?"

"I'm not talking to you," she said firmly.

"He just said he's having an appointment with adventure. Does that sound like normal conversation to you? "

"Big deal. It means leave him alone, and while you're at it, take that mound of mash potatoes off your thumb."

Had to love my mom. The woman was the best.

Rodgers and Hammerstein (Key of B)

"They wanted to know if you could sing," so said my manager.

"Tell Rodgers and Hammerstein to check with Danny Kaye. He'll give them the straight scoop on that one," I replied.

"They're really interested in you. They said you don't need to have a great voice."

I just knew I would never hear the end of this from my father if I didn't follow through. So I grudgingly allowed my manager to talk me into auditioning for their new Broadway musical. After taking just two singing lessons (from a guy who farted repeatedly without any sign of embarrassment), I found myself backstage with about fifty or more young performers, all waiting to do their thing.

As I signed in, I noticed my hand was a little shaky. Definitely some tension involved, mostly because I was presenting the weakest part of my talent. I could dance, but the singing part was not a confidence builder. I began to regret showing up, when suddenly a voice said, "I'm really nervous. How about you?"
I turned and found a girl so pretty and so eager to

connect that she thrust her hands into mine. "Feel my hands. They're like ice."

I melted on the spot. All my nerves disappeared in one smitten moment. I had arrived at the audition feeling a little under the weather, probably running some sort of temperature, so I placed her hands on my cheeks to warm them up. She thought that was such a sweet gesture, she practically cooed. With genuine belief, I told her that once out on stage, she would be so fabulous she'd surprise herself. I must have sounded like a sage, because it steadied her to such a degree, she was amazed, and thanked me profusely.

But the more we hit it off, the more I thought about what lay ahead. How could I go out there with what I had to offer? It didn't help that every performer that had gone on was so stellar, they could have landed the lead role in *A Star Is Born*. I had to get her phone number and run the crap out of there as fast as I could. Too late! Just at that moment, my name was called. I quickly looked around, searching for someone with the odd name of Joey Walsh, when my dream girl busted me. "That's you!" she said excitedly. When she added "break a leg", I only wished she had a hammer to complete the deed.

I don't remember how I got to the middle of that stage without being carried out, but there I was telling the piano player I would be singing 'You Make Me Feel So Young'. Since I didn't bring sheet music (unheard of), he asked, "In what key?" I was stumped. Bless his heart, he could spot trouble and suggested key of B. I quickly recovered and said, "B's good." Now here's where I deserved some credit. When the chips were down, I NEVER SANG THE SONG BETTER—and it still stunk.

A deafening silence filled the space...followed by the solemn words, "Thank you."

It was over. Humiliation complete. THEN—believe it or not, out of my mouth came the immortal words, "I have a little dance number."

Even though I didn't hear it, I could feel a gasp come from the darkened theater. As for the kids backstage, I could only imagine them rolling around the floor, clutching their ribs, with my lady-love sadly watching. Nevertheless, I asked the pianist to play, 'Once In Love with Amy', a number made famous by the funky dancing of the scarecrow in *The Wizard of Oz*. To top it off, I suggested he play the song in the key of B.

The piano player looked at me for one long bemused moment, then said, "Why not. Key of B it is, boss."

He must have taken great pity on me not to laugh out loud. I'm sure no one before needed a key of any kind to perform a dance number. (Hopefully, the pianist has gotten a lot of mileage out of retelling the Key of B story through the years...I know I have.) But at the time, whatever image I carried about myself had left town. Basic survival was the issue.

How could I get past a horde of fellow performers trying to sneak a peek at what true disaster looked like. Eye contact had to be avoided at all costs. Most of all by the pretty girl that would never be.

I Should Be Dead

Needless to say, after such a gut wrenching audition, I wasn't too thrilled with my manager. He knew I could barely sing, but still pushed me hard to perform for the two giants of musical theater. Rodgers and Hammerstein had seen the best of the best, and there I was. Basically a lamb being led to you-know-what. Where was my protection? It wasn't the manager's psyche being served up for ridicule.

This was the mindset that showed up at Roy's that night. With a pocket full of past winnings, I was looking to play the guy considered to be the best barrel pin bowler in this god-forsaken hell hole.

Through his squint-like gaze, Tangerine measured me for any 'tell' of vulnerability he could find. Then said, "How many pins do you want, lucky?"

"None," I said. "Even money."

Instantly, this dead ass place came alive. Did they hear right? Is he really going to take on Tangerine with NO SPOT?! EVEN MONEY? Tangerine himself showed no reaction. Mr. Cool. Then reached down and removed his bowling ball. Not the traditional black ball used by everyone else. His was yellow with a hint of tangerine in it. Everyone else saw the color red as the sharks moved in.

As I expected, money poured in on Tangerine from every shady pocket. While covering all bets, I tried telling myself I was taking a shot at some real money. But was that really the reason for my behavior? Something else was going on, but I never bothered to examine it. At the time, I was pretty good at that.

Driven to play great, I bowled the best I ever had and he still beat me by ONE LOUSY PIN! I knew I should have quit right there, or gotten a favorable handicap, but I had a date with destiny that couldn't be shaken. As I lost game after game, the whole place was out for my blood. Shrieking, howling, and saying rotten things.

One particular guy who I had never seen before, kept repeating the same thing, "Hey kid, what do you want to lay me?" He was slurring his words and probably had too much to drink, so I was doing my best to ignore him. But…combined with the losing, he was really getting on my nerves. I was the goddamn underdog in the match! Asking me to give him the best of the price was so beyond stupid, I finally snapped.

"You I'll lay!" I meant it in terms of a fight. Like in, 'you I'll lay out.' By me missing the word 'out', he must have taken it in a sexual way, because he immediately sobered, broke his beer bottle, and came savagely slashing at my face. He missed by just a fraction. Fortunately for me, I had the bowling ball in my hand and in self-defense threw it at point blank range in his face. It hit his throat area, forcing him to drop his jagged beer bottle. Gulping for air, he staggered out of control until he reached the exit, and left. It all happened so fast and violently that I could barely register it in my brain.

All I could hear was Lefty telling me to get out of there quick because he knew the guy, and he was certain to get a gun and come back to kill me. Normally, Lefty and urgency didn't belong in the same sentence. He was as laid back as they come, but at this moment he was rattled and deadly serious. His reaction actually shook me.

Everything in me wanted to do what Lefty said, but all I could hear myself say was, "Fuck'em".

Running off was just a 'no go'. I understood and felt fear, but my actions never felt like a hard choice. Better to go out feeling like a man or some bullshit like that. Ego and pride in full arrogance. In retrospect, I knew I was a horse's ass, but at that moment I would face the consequences.

Alone at Roy's bar many hours later, I looked past the cracked mirror toward daybreak, then downed another shot of whisky with a beer chaser. Somewhere in the echos of my mind I could hear my father, 'Turned out to be a fuckin' bum.'

Yep pops, you were right, sit down and have a boilermaker with me, and lets shoot the shit. Tell me all the glowing things you feel about my career. Don't hold back anything. Feel free to tell me what a colossal disappointment I turned out to be. Tell me how I threw away everything. All your hopes and dreams killed by your kid. Let's get it all out, Pa. I got all the time in the world because I ain't going anywhere. Yeah, I said— ain't, Pa. You can take the kid out of the street, but you can't take the street out of the kid. Sorry if I screwed up all you ever wanted, I know how that feels. I wanted to be the welterweight champ of the world, but you nixed that. Who could blame you. What parent wanted to see their kid get hurt. Still, it was my dream, replaced by yours. I just couldn't get as excited about it as you were.

I was stuck in that gloom and doom scenario when in walked THE GUY. Lefty was right, but I wouldn't listen. Now I was going to die in this shit-hole, lowlife dump. I knew it beyond a shadow of a doubt. As he headed straight for me, my initial fear gave way to intense anger. I suddenly found myself rising and heading for this guy with such directness and fury in my heart that it was scary. I knew his hand would be coming out of his overcoat pocket any second, and I was just going to be there, and break him and the gun in half.

Somehow this crazed truth must have translated, because when we were within feet of each other, his eyes, which were locked into mine, lost their certainty and lowered to the floor. As he brushed past, I was amazed by my own restraint at not attacking him, because every fiber in my body was ready for a fight to the death. I knew it would be just moments before he turned to gun me down. With my eyes glued on him, I backed my way toward the exit as he approached a pool table, picked up the Eight-ball, stared at it, and that was it. I was gone.

Leaving Town

Hours later, after my third cup of black coffee, I still couldn't shake the Roy's bowling alley experience. Facing death twice in a one evening was difficult for my brain to sort out. A close call like that should force you into action, but I didn't want to think about it. Just wanted to sit there and slow it down. Remove the drama for the time being. Drink coffee till I felt like a normal person. It was through this mixed up brain muddle that I glanced up at the diner's wall clock. It was exactly 12 o'clock. Was it a sign? Get out of town before someone comes to kill me? Lost in that Gary Cooper *'High Noon'* scenario, a tap on my shoulder really startled me. As I quickly turned to confront, I was met by the smiling face of a guy I played softball with in the Broadway Show League.

He apologized for scaring me like that, and I just dismissed it as no problem. As we chatted, he told me he wouldn't be at Thursday's softball game because that's the day he was driving off to California. He had quit his job as a Broadway stagehand, bought himself a brand new Cadillac, and was heading out west to try his hand at what he called...the 'acting bit'.

He wondered if I knew anybody who would like to come along and split the driving chores. I didn't hesitate. "Other than me, don't know of anyone else."

He was blown away by my response. Wanted to know if I was kidding him, because he still thought of me as some big name TV actor. When he realized I was dead serious, he was crazy with delight. Kept saying he couldn't get over his good fortune at running into me. I barely heard anything else, because my mind was racing ahead with a minor problem. I'd never driven a car. Luckily, there were a few days to learn. I knew a guy from my neighborhood who had an old stick-shift. Two hours later, I was being given my first and only driving lesson.

The following day, I was sitting behind the wheel of his beat up car, ready to take my driving test. Naturally, I was feeling a little nervous, and to make matters worse, ran into a test guy who wasn't built to make anyone feel comfortable. No hello. No smile. Seriously abrupt. Constantly wincing in discomfort. He got into the passenger seat, and immediately barked out, "My fucking broken toe is aching like shit. Lets get this done."

Well, that was it for me. My mind turned to so much mush I couldn't even remember how to start the car. Stalling for time, I stuck my face out the window for what seemed like four months, looking to my left for oncoming traffic. There was nothing coming on the street, or in my head.

Panic rising, I stuck out my arm, indicating to the non-coming traffic I'm about to pull out, when the test guy growls, "What the hell are you waiting for!?"

Surprisingly, this helps, because just like that I remember how to start the car.

I'm still pretty stiff, and driving along super careful, when he says, "Don't you ever shift?"

Christ! I forgot the shift part of it. I make an excuse that I was trying to build up more speed before I did, but okay, shifting a little sooner would be more than fine by me. Thanks for the tip. I was trying my best to get him on my side, but this bad-toed bastard was having no part of it. Before long he had me drive into this empty enclosure that was as wide and long as a football field. After a few minor instructions, he asked me to make a U-turn.

It was my first U, and would prove to be my last until two years later. I began by making the 'slowest and widest' turn imaginable, but still was about to run into a fence, so I stopped.

"Did I ask you for a broken U," the guy said irritably.

Thinking quickly, I replied, "Oh, did you just want a simple U?"

He didn't say a word, but made some sort of eerie sound, followed by, "BACK-THE-CAR-UP-AND-FAST."

His elaborate, measured tone, told me he wasn't pleased. That made two of us. My mind had become so crowded with hatred for the car and test guy, I accidentally stepped too hard on the gas petal and we flew backward at breakneck speed. Broken toe and all, he desperately stretched out to reach the brake petal so widely, he strained his groin.

I gave him a few 'sorry, sorry', but he just said, "Get out of the car. Get out of the car. GET OUT OF THE FUCKING CAR!"

After we traded seats, he immediately launched into a tirade. "Let me tell you how badly you failed. I-HAVE-NEVER-BEEN-INVOLVED-IN-A-MORE-MISERABLE-TEST-THAN-THIS-ONE."

Not willing to accept any more of his abuse, I told him that the people down at the DMV said the test guy wasn't allowed to say if you passed or failed. That it would only come by mail.

"In your case I made an exception," he said, "No suspense needed." That was actually a pretty funny retort, but I wouldn't give this prick the benefit of the laugh.

Come early Thursday morning, I took off in the passenger seat of the stagehand's brand new Caddy, bound for Los Angeles. It was good I left the Big Apple when I did, because my father told me his insides were for the shits, and that he couldn't handle one more day of watching his health go down the drain over me. Whatever the medical report, the truth was, both father and son were badly in need of a vacation from each other.

With no license, and no fanfare awaiting me at some Hollywood train station, the conditions had really changed since the last time I headed west. This time I was in *Escape from New York* mode, trying to up my chances of reaching age twenty-one. I was alive, at least, and had a shot at turning it all around. Thankfully the stagehand liked to drive, so my turn behind the wheel wasn't all that demanding. Plus driving an automatic rather than a stick-shift was a piece of cake.

Eating anything however, including jello, became a whole different story. Somehow along the way I had developed a serious gum infection called Trench mouth. Consuming any food or water became a major ordeal. I thought it was because I hadn't brushed my teeth enough during the cross country trip, but the ER doctor in New Mexico wasn't in agreement.

Dr. Hurt (his real name) asked a pointed but surprising question. "Have you been under some unusual stress lately?" Wow, how the hell did he come up with that?!

Even though he was a friendly enough guy, I didn't want to go into past history with him, so I mumbled through painful lips, "Nothing to write home about."

But boy was I impressed with Dr. Hurt. That was before he slashed my hugely swollen gums. Two seconds for the top and two seconds for the bottom. Four seconds of bad blood flying on me...Him...and the Nurse standing near by. She actually let out a little scream. Then quickly cupped her mouth. It was a heart-stopping attack on a scale not invented yet; one that produced an out of world pain experience. He was fortunate there wasn't a scalpel nearby to fight back.

When I was back in the car and heading for the Golden State, I started thinking that the bad blood left behind was a sign that things would get better from here on in. Getting a sip of water down without wincing in pain was a promising start. I was trying my best to pump up the old confidence level, because I still had to face the unknown, with very little money and fewer prospects.

Oh Captain! My Captain!

All the New York actors that moved to Hollywood were working like crazy, so everybody thought that with my early credits, it was a cinch I'd be back on top before long. As my father pointed out, Jimmy Dean had become a monster star, and when Jimmy and I played brothers on TV, I'd walked off with all the reviews. I never saw these so-called reviews, so I didn't know what he was talking about. For some reason, Dad was still envious of Dean's career, even though he'd already payed the ultimate price for his short lived fame. It certainly wasn't Dean's fault I didn't rocket to stardom.

Despite my phone not ringing off the hook with job offers, I felt I was in the right place. Where New York had become a tight squeeze in more ways than one, California felt open and uncluttered. A place big enough to take a deep breath and start fresh. I could walk down a street, pick an orange off a tree and nobody cared. Things were there for the taking if I would just give it time.

Thanks to the insistence of the stagehand, I was living rent free in his apartment. Although, it was clear I was just an investment to him. He felt it was only a matter of time before I was back in a key position, and able to help him with the 'acting bit'. Socially we went our separate ways, which was plenty alright by me. Being alone led to many a Fred Astaire revival, so I was always in good company. Fred always made life such a pleasure to behold, there was no way to feel down while watching him. Such a gift.

Eventually though, I heard about a place just right for me. This led to 'nighttime at the Raincheck'. I know—sounds like a song just waiting for a lyric. Lots of hopes and dreams in the form of out-of-work actors, nursing a beer and eager for the free chili. Besides Mr. Astaire, this place was a tonic for getting through the night, knowing full well the day was just around the corner.. and starting to get longer despite my positive attitude. Being yesterday's news sure wasn't any fun, so it was good I found a second home. Before long, I recruited a bunch of the Raincheck crowd to join the Entertainment Softball League. It would prove to be a turning point for me on a number of levels.

One bright morning (keep the word bright in your back pocket for now), I was having breakfast at Schwab's in Hollywood—possibly the world's most famous drugstore. A place where Charlie Chaplin once made his own sodas, and starlets awaited discovery. I had no illusions about rediscovery. I was there strictly because the food was great.

As I left Schwab's for my first softball practice, some

fast-talking, ultra jittery guy pulls me aside and tries to sell me a beautifully packaged suede vest. I knew the type well. Many of them were always up at Roy's Bowling Alley, plying their 'shady business deals'. They would steal anything you wanted, and sell it to you at one-fourth the list price. Whatever was needed would be gotten to you fast. I would always respond the same way. "Thanks, I'm good today. But maybe some other time."

Keeping things polite, and possible, was always the wiser choice at Roy's, even though I had no intentions of ever getting involved with this crew. That was until the day I saw 'them.' So soft, so beautiful, and with my Mom's birthday coming in a week, I had to have those gorgeous brown leather gloves. They sold for $115, and I got them for $25. I was always savvy when it came to making a good deal.

But coming out of Schwab's that day, the world was in a whole different place for me. For starters, I wasn't in need of a suede vest, nor did I have funds to spend on such a luxury. The 'booster' (thief) was offering eighty five percent off the list price. It really was such a sweet deal, I hesitated for a split second. That's all it took. He went into hard drive, acting frantically as if police were about to nab him.

"Forget it," he said, and quickly turned to leave.

Just as quick, I countered, "Ninety percent off and you got a deal."

He paused with annoyance..."Gimme the money FAST."

As I quickly paid him, he saw the sixty bucks I had left, and shoved the whole twelve vests into my arms.

"Gimme the other sixty, and they're all yours. FAST. FAST."

I gave him the dough, and like a good thief should, he was gone in a flash. My only thought now, was to get to my four hundred dollar crappy car before the police nailed me with 'hot' merchandise. When I was safely behind the wheel, I barely had time to think of my big score when I suddenly became aware of a police car not far behind me. Oh Shit. Think fast. 'Hey guys, I didn't know the vests were stolen? How would I know that? You're looking at an honest to goodness victim here.'

As I was rehearsing my tone with various degrees of realism, the police car turned at the next corner. What a relief. I didn't have to 'act' my way out of a bad situation. Even though safe—never once did I stop rehearsing till I got to the ball field. Whether I was practicing acting, or survival, it was a relief to just let it go. The thought of going to jail over twelve unneeded

108

suede vests felt sorta dumb, but there was another part of me that liked not becoming a chicken shit and passing up such a bargain. I was twelve deep wealthy in suede. Somebody was in for a nice present and I felt good about that.

I was about to unwrap my super classy vest, when it struck me again how beautifully packaged it was. Everything about it said 'please don't disturb my elegance'. Maybe I should wait till I got home and get the full mirror effect. That way I could try on different attitudes, while checking myself out at various angles. Nah, couldn't wait. So with the air of a country gentleman, I carefully opened my prize, and THERE IT WAS! A suede front—and that's it! No back whatsoever!!

How could this happen to me? A kid from the big city! My God, if New Yorkers ever found out one of their own had turned into such a putz, they'd be thrilled I'd left. There was really no reason to open another package because I knew the story, but I did anyhow. What a complete hustle. I had to give the thief credit for his stellar performance. My performance on the other hand, should be buried away, never to be talked about, until I was at least a 100 and people suspected dementia.

Yet the more I thought about it, the more it made me

smile. Why not present each of my new teammates with their very own 1/2 vests? After all, I was going to be their captain. Why leave any doubt as to what shrewd management would look like. I can't begin to tell you the power of laughter. I've never been on a team that came together faster.

We were a scrappy bunch of actors, playing against other teams that definitely had more name value. One in particular was a team paid and clothed by actor James Garner, which he called 'The Leading Men'. Since we, and many other teams, were comprised of many out of work character actors, I felt a little more sensitivity on Garner's part might have been in order in choosing a team name. But it was his money, so he could do what he wanted.

When it came our turn to compete against The Leading Men, it turned into more than just a softball game. While playing shortstop, the ball was hit to me with the bases loaded. As I was about to throw home for the force out, I went flying through the air, landing with a heavy thud to the ground, glasses broken, courtesy of actor James Garner. Of course I knew he was going to be called out and all, but still I was upset because everybody knows you don't barrel into the shortstop in that situation.

So as I'm lying in the dirt, trying to forgive him for not knowing how to play, I hear Garner bellow, "Next time that guy gets in my way, I'll break his back."

I couldn't believe what I just heard! It brought up such fury that despite my body feeling the effect of the blow, I was on my feet in a moment, and charged Garner for all I was worth. He retreated so fast to center field, that despite him calling his team 'The Leading Men', anyone would have major difficulty casting him as a hero anytime soon. It took almost my whole team to physically restrain me. Needless to say, his show *Maverick* never held much charm for me.

WTF!

A few days after the softball incident, I found myself
sitting in an office waiting to audition for a Prell
Shampoo commercial. I knew my audition was going to
be a stiff. It called for great excitement, how Prell had
changed my life. There was no way I could supply the
'gushing' needed, so I decided to leave. Why waste
their time and create an embarrassment for both of us.

On my way out, a hand locked onto my wrist, "So I
heard you chased Garner into the cow pasture."

The voice belonged to Larry 'Bud' Pernell, a guy I knew
from the softball league. Bud was once a professional
ballplayer for the Boston Braves, who had turned to
acting. I didn't want to get into the Garner story so
dismissed it as just one of those things.

"You're not going to do this Prell crap, right?"

I just told him I wasn't right for the part, and Bud said
he felt the same way and should leave. He didn't.
Instead, he pressed to meet later for a drink, at a place
down the street that served great Sangrias. This was
the last thing I wanted to do. First of all I wasn't into
afternoon drinking, and knew this was just going to turn
into a tale of woe that I was looking to avoid. It was

112

tough enough to stay positive the way things were going. But Bud appeared so sincerely depressed I couldn't say no. This wouldn't turn out well for either of us.

As we sat drinking Sangrias, with Bud lamenting about show business, a man approached our table rather aggressively. Except for eyes and mouth, his entire face and head was covered in gauze. The guy seemed to be under the impression we were saying bad things about him, and wanted to know what our problem was.

This dude was putting out such a weird vibe that I wanted no part of him.

"What the hell are you talking about," said Bud. "Just sit down and drink Sangria with us."

He did. That was about 1PM. He left us at 1AM. After hitting numerous bars courtesy of Bud, the man who had barely uttered a word for twelve hours, decided to become belligerent again. Told Bud he didn't approve of all his drinking and bar-hopping.

That's all it took. Bud rose up in his drunkenness—all 6'2", 230 pounds of him—and said at a deafening level, "Get the hell out of here, you fucking mummy!"

Wisely, the mummy disappeared. Never did find out who he was or why the bandages. It was not a night for getting to know you. Zero camaraderie attached to it. Just an endless blur of bars requesting we take our business elsewhere.

Bud driving half on the street and half on people's lawns, should have been a clue to the condition I was in, because I don't remember registering a complaint about it. Thank god the police were on the job. Their flashing red lights shining right behind us astonished Bud. Why in the world were they stopping him?

As the police followed us into a gas station, Bud was still puzzled what the problem could be. He was so intoxicated, he couldn't fathom why they asked him to walk a straight line.

"You guys don't think I'm drunk, do you?" he said in a barely intelligible slur.

"Just walk, sir," one cop replied.

Bud was barely able to stand up, let alone walk a straight line, so I tried to intervene on his behalf. All I managed to get out was, "Listen, guys," at which point the other cop snapped at me: "Don't say another word or we'll lock you up too." He ordered me to back up and don't stand close to them. As loaded as I was, I knew enough to abide with their demand.

114

As I stood back, the whole day and night started to close in on me. My eyelids grew heavy. About to nod off, I suddenly caught a glimpse of the two cops charging at me. They were coming with such intensity, I could do nothing but spread my legs wide to brace for a serious takedown. Instead, they ran right past, got into their police car and screeched off through a red light, disappearing into a surreal evening.

As I'm trying to piece together what had just happened, I hear Bud's voice and turn toward him. Oblivious to the fact that the cops were gone, he's telling them about some strange Mummy they should be on the look out for, rather than making him walk some STUPID WHITE LINE.

My Favorite Martian

God knows how I got home, but morning left me even more mystified. I had lost the heels on both my boots. What in the world?? I called Bud to get the story. Had we been involved in some kind of incredible brawl? He didn't have a clue. All he knew was that he had arrived home on four rims and no tires.

This was not good. I didn't come to Hollywood to spend a 'lost evening' with a depressed big leaguer, hostile mummy, and a hangover to end all hangovers. Things had to change, but how?

While pondering a dubious future, my agent called with a suggestion. Maybe I should consider finding new representation. Someone who'd have better luck with me. This was just the type of call to bolster one's confidence, but I refused to let it throw me. Quite calmly, I told him there was no way I would ever leave him because I liked him too much. How could I live with myself once I became a big money earner and saw those HUGE commissions go to some other agent?

For his part, he was willing to take that chance. That was just fear talking, I said. Turn downs were just a test of one's true colors, and even if he didn't know it, everyone that knew him had said he was a fighter, and

116

that's the only reason I signed with him. In actuality, there was not one person I spoke with who had ever heard of this agent.

I don't know why I was clinging to this guy, but I could see I was making some mental inroads with him, so I threw in a novel idea. Even though he was earning ten percent of nothing, I suggested he loan me some money to protect his interest. With that, he swallowed wrong and broke into a coughing fit, unable to speak.

I pressed forward, "The agent-paying-the-actor isn't the norm, I get that, but that's the beauty of it. For a few hundred bucks, you could become a legend in this town, rather than a perceived blood sucker."

Once he recovered, he agreed to $150—under one stipulation: If I didn't land the next job he sent me on, it would terminate our relationship without another word spoken. What could I do? I accepted. Shortly thereafter, the moment of truth arrived. It was a TV show called, *My Favorite Martian.* I got the job!

My actor friends in the Raincheck rejoiced, and in celebration bought me the first Martini I ever had. In fact, they kept buying me Martini's, which I didn't particularly care for, but loved the olives. When the following day arrived my whole body felt obliterated.

I was sick as a dog, but somehow managed to make it to the studio.

Lucky for me it was a read through day, rather than a shooting day. No way was I able to get through the read. I was throwing up so badly, the producers had to send me to the studio doctor. My body was in shock. The doctor asked me if I had been drinking the night before. I felt certain if I'd said "Yes Doc, I had sixteen Martinis," my Hollywood career would be over before it began. I claimed bad sausage at breakfast as the culprit. I knew he didn't really believe me, and with the studio calling and pressuring him whether they should recast, my chances of surviving this was dubious.

Everything told me he wasn't about to put his career on the line (nor should he), so I made a crazy gamble and told the truth. The celebration, the Martinis, the agent that was going to call it quits—the whole works! I threw myself at the mercy of a stranger who only had one obligation, and that wasn't to me.

As his phone rang, our eyes held each others until he picked up the receiver. I braced, Please God… "Hello, this is Dr. Josephs,"…A short beat that felt like an eternity followed, then…"Well, he had some bad sausage for breakfast. I suspect a little case of food poisoning, but if I send him home now, he'll be good to go in the morning."

I exhaled, and wordlessly said, 'thank you God.' With that, Dr. Josephs turned to me and said, "You're welcome," then hung up the phone. Maybe it was his office lighting or my grade D vision, but I swear it looked like he had a halo around him.

Interacting with Gregory Peck

After *My Favorite Martian*, work remained scarce. A few more TV shows here and there, but not enough to survive. It was at that point I was invited to play poker. The buy in was two hundred bucks. I happened to have two hundred and two dollars left in the world, so why not take a shot. Didn't have that much experience as a poker player, so coming up a loser was likely, but it was a gamble I felt I had to take.

That evening I played like I was made for the game, and won six hundred bucks! Poker, where have you been all my life?! Looking back, it should have been no surprise that a game of chance would be my go-to. Risking for me was like breathing. It came easily. It was part of my makeup even when I was unaware of it. I didn't consider myself brave because I took risks; on the contrary, many times I thought what the hell am I doing? I was smart enough to know how stupid my choices were at times, but it was okay. I'll learn. I had faith. There was no inclination to make a big deal over my shortcomings. If life took a bad turn, then hey, that's on me.

Poker games were everywhere, and every night. And even though I wasn't getting rich, they were helping, along with a few TV jobs, to just barely keep my head above water.

When I landed a part in a movie called *Captain Newman M.D.*, it was a thankful bonus. A smallish role, but my scenes were with major star, Gregory Peck, so that was nice. Peck played a medical Army doctor in charge of a psych ward and I was one of his war-traumatized patients. The way my career had bottomed out, I thought it was good casting.

Acting with the likes of Gregory Peck was a trip, but interacting off screen with him was a revelation. This incredibly caring, searching, down to earth man was a worried soul. He voiced his concern for his sons and their direction in life. He seemed to have me down as some well-adjusted young man who knew who he was —why he was here— and where he was going. I felt like looking over my shoulder to make sure he was talking about yours truly. I didn't want to disappoint, nor burst his bubble, so I never mentioned how I had arrived that morning from an all-night poker game where I won a few bucks, while also scoring a new bookmaker. Certainly a nice parlay for me, but if Gregory was looking for words of wisdom for his kids, I didn't have much to offer.

Some years later, I read that Peck's first son, Jonathan, stuck a gun to his temple and killed himself at age thirty. Wow. It was tough to get my head around it. My mind kept tripping back to the day I worked on *Captain Newman.* So many questions. Why would

Gregory Peck share his personal troubles with me? Being a major movie star didn't stop him from being a vulnerable human being. Saving his sons from whatever they were going through was all that mattered to him. What did he think I knew that could have made a difference?

Maybe if I had gone a little deeper into my own difficulties, I might have left him with something. He was clearly reaching out, but I didn't know how to reach within. I wasn't at that point in my life, but he seemed to think I was. In that way, I feel I failed him. Not that I believe I could have changed events, but really wished I could have been more helpful to the real Atticus Finch.

Stardom, Here I Come Again

After *Captain Newman*, nothing of import happened that would generate a career surge. I was still scraping by playing winning poker and collecting unemployment checks, but there was a rebellion brewing. Two of my fellow actors and I were getting fed up with our agents rarely calling. So we decided to take our hostile feelings out on the golf course, driving vicious ground balls and hideous slices.

One day, a foursome playing behind us asked if they could play ahead. Now we knew our game wasn't quite up to par, and normally would have said yes to the request, but the guy asking said it in such a shitty, put-down manner, my answer came back, "No. Wait your turn."

After teeing off, I headed toward my second shot, when a golf ball came whizzing inches past my head with such force, it could easily have killed. I was ticked off by this guy earlier — Now I couldn't see straight. This dude's move was so wildly wrong and dangerous that I immediately picked up a golf club and started toward him with furious intent.

The closer I got, the faster he back-peddled, yelling, "I'm a Karate Master..I'm a Karate Master..Don't come near me. I'm a Karate Master."

I would've needed track shoes to reach this fearless Karate Master, so the situation ended without further incident. I guess the moral of the story is, never rile up an out-of-work actor.

In the retelling of this, my buddies said that when I first went for the guy, I had abruptly stopped and come back to replace my nine iron for a seven, because I felt I needed more club. Don't remember that, and still refuse to believe it.

Anyway, we soldiered on at the golf course for a few more months until one of our threesome turned into a 'deserter.' As we came to pick him up, he was sitting in a really shabby, GODAWFUL bathrobe in his crappy yard, appearing to write a screenplay. He said some nonsense about attending to a career, so he had to cut us loose. Wasn't very sporting of him, but I suspect Jack Nicholson made the right decision. Turns out the screenplay was made into a movie called *Head*, and starred The Monkeys.

Knowing money was always a key issue for me, Jack got the movie company to offer me a day's work. My whole role was to hand a town mayor a pair of scissors, so he could cut a ceremonial ribbon. It was

124

basically a glorified extra. Oh, how the mighty had fallen. They offered $125 for the day. I told them I'd do it for $200 and would bring my own scissors free of charge. I felt a little humor would ease the hatred the company was showing for clearly being extorted on the price.

It's tough to believe that after that experience, things could get more disheartening, but they did. My unemployment benefits had run out, and I had cooled off at the poker table. Even the golf fees, which were practically nothing on the public course, were harder and harder to muster up.

Then one day, out of the blue, destiny struck. I nailed a birdie on the eighth hole. Being a real animal lover, I rescued the badly limping dove and brought it into the club house for emergency care. It seemed like the moment I walked in, the phone rang. Within seconds, I heard my name mentioned. My agent was on the phone, frantically trying to find me. I couldn't believe it. I had to report to United Artist Studio immediately for a wardrobe fitting, because I was due to start filming the following day. I would be playing the part of Billy in the movie, *Invitation To A Gunfighter,* starring Yul Brynner and George Segal.

Even though my agent had told me he submitted my name to play the part of Billy the Kid, I never really gave it much of a shot since my has-been status was under a full head of steam. This was a miracle. Yet in some strange Hollywood way, I could see how it might have happened last minute: Lead actor drops out - boom. They pull out my picture - boom. See that I got the look - boom. Pull the trigger - boom boom. Stardom, here I come again.

Billy the Kid

Naturally I was overjoyed, but tried to keep a lid on it, because I could only imagine what my golfing actor buddy, Mark (Butch) Cavell must be feeling. He wasn't setting the show business community on fire either. I told him I was sorry about screwing up his golfing day, but swore to god I would be taking him to the top with me.

At wardrobe, they started me out with an extra large, red-checkered shirt that looked like a burlap sack. I expressed some doubt about it nicely, but they really liked it. I glanced toward Butch, who sort of shrugged. I could tell he was on the same page as me.

Next, wardrobe put me in an oversized pair of trousers. Chuckling, I told them I could fit two of me in the outfit, and still have room for my friend Butch to climb in. Butch laughed, but 'wardrobe' looked pretty serious. They didn't see what was wrong. In fact, they thought the pants looked perfect. I could see Butchie's face from the corner of my eye, cracking a little smile. He could clearly see what I saw. A buffoon. After snapping on some clownish red suspenders, they topped off the whole thing by adorning my head with a rounded cowboy hat, very similar to the one that Dan Blocker used in the old *Bonanza* series.

Butch didn't know whether to laugh or cry, but I knew, as a leading actor in the movie, the time had come to speak up. The last thing I wanted to look like was a temperamental actor; but after finally getting my big break again, I was damned if I would let myself be laughed off the silver screen.

I started with the hat, removing it decisively. "Forget the hat, boys. It just ain't me." Dancing as fast as I could, I went to work on the pants, lying that my hobby was fast gun competition. I demonstrated how my quick draw would be hitting nothing but flap. It would look ridiculous, not to mention slowing me down. In my mind, I couldn't let go of how sleek and fabulous movie star Robert Taylor looked playing *Billy The Kid*. I told the guys I was leaning more to tight black leather— something dapper, dark and deadly. I waited a brief second for a reply. From the blankness of their expression I could see I wasn't getting through to them.

"Look guys, I'm not trying to be a prima donna pain in the ass here, but I'm the one that has to play this role. I'm the one that has to feel comfortable, and constantly hitting 'flap' just ain't going to do it for me."

They looked at each other, then back at me, but said nothing.

Uncomfortably, I continued with my next lie. "I'm also a western history buff, and even though I know that the character wasn't the brightest guy in the world, I still can't play him as a goofball. Sorry if I'm causing you trouble...But I just can't see myself playing Billy the Kid in this outfit."

There was a pause. "Billy the Kid?" said one wardrobe guy with a straight face. "You're playing Billy the clerk."

I don't recall how long it took me to sink to the floor, but I do remember being curled up in a fetal position. Without looking up, I told wardrobe not to worry. I just needed to lie there for a while.

Butch, who was having difficulty stifling laughter, now began to read one of my two lines in the movie: (STAGE DIRECTION) Billy the clerk emits a gooney cackle before saying to the gunfighter, "Can I take your luggage?" My other memorable line was something like —"It's room 210."

Without uttering another word, wardrobe decided to change my outfit. I guess they felt bad for me. Either that or they didn't want to be held responsible for a potential bridge-leaper.

Hee-Hee-Hee

After leaving the studio in a numbed state, I turned to Butch, who was trying hard to maintain the integrity of my crushed silence. "Butch, I know something about this is very funny, and somewhere down the line, maybe way down, we'll be able to laugh about it. But right now, I would rather you didn't mention this to anyone."

He swore up and down he knew exactly how I felt, and that I could depend on him. The following day I received a call from an actor I knew, who immediately launched into a song that Butch, my good and loyal friend, had composed. "He's Billy the clerk... A lurking jerk... He lurks and lurks," etc, etc...

After three similar musical calls from different 'friends', I refused to answer the phone anymore. I knew that was probably being a poor sport about the whole thing, but needed time to recover. I still had to face Billy, the lurking jerk in the morning, and that wasn't going to be easy. What I didn't anticipate—was just how difficult it was going to be.

The following day I met Yul Brynner. It wasn't the first time. Before he was given his life-changing role in the *King and I* on Broadway, he had directed me in a starring role in early New York TV. Even for a kid of thirteen, Mr. Brynner wasn't your every day type. Not only for the bald head and dramatic look, but for the way he approached each morning. He would bring in a little Victrola and play Edith Piaf, singing *La Vie En Rose* before starting rehearsal. It certainly was different and because of him, I grew to love the sound of Piaf's voice. I thought by mentioning this, it would be a nice surprise for him, plus seeing me all grown up. I must have been dreaming, because he faked remembrance, then dismissed me all together. Big stars and present-day bit players are a bad mix.

Worse still—was the movie's director's vision of how my two line part should be played. I had planned to disappear in the role, and he insisted I stand out. So much so, that it caused quite a bit of tension. What he wanted from me, I just couldn't seem to deliver. Namely over-the-top HEE-HEE-HEES just at the sight of Yul Brynner's gun. I must have been feeling some inner resistance because take after take I tried all kinds of self-conscious laughter. Take after take he yelled, "Cut," followed by, "No! No!! No!!!"

Eventually he grew hostile, got right up in my face and basically screamed, "I told you I want HEE-HEE-HEES. HEE-HEE-HEES, damn it!!" With that, he abruptly turned away and said let's do it again. Left with embarrassment, bordering on humiliation, all I could think was - it's good Yul Brynner didn't remember me.

Finally, mercifully, the director said, "Print. Let's move on."

I could tell by the sheer disgust on his face I had failed him miserably. I was able to give him a couple of hee-hees, possibly even a hee-hee and a haw, but three hee hee hee's were obviously beyond my range. Being out of work for so long had taken quite a toll on my craft. As the director moved off with his movie star, I heard him say, "I'm sorry, Yul. I don't know what casting was thinking of..." It's good I didn't hear the rest, because he'd fast become a prime candidate for my sneaky-but-lethal-left-hook.

Bad Beat

After *Invitation to a Gunfighter*, there was no flood of
job offers, so it was back to the poker scene, playing
day after day in both clubs and private games. Luckily,
I was winning more than losing. That was important
because in the interim, I met a nice girl, said 'I do,' and
waited to see if show business would ever say hello
again.

The good-byes were all too frequent and discouraging,
until one day I met with the director Robert Wise, who
was casting a huge movie called *The Sand Pebbles*.
We hit it off great. After leaving, I felt there was a real
shot to land one of the ship's crew. None of the sailor
parts were going to be that meaningful, but it was
going to be a five month shoot in the South China
seas. And *nothing* could have sounded better to me at
the time.

Not only would the weekly paycheck be a god-send,
but escaping Los Angeles and heading for the China
seas began to take on life-saving proportions. The
more I thought about it, the more anxious I became,
and being in need that much was really disturbing. I felt
off balance. How would I recover if this didn't work

out? My mind was doing it's best scare job, and doing it well enough to weaken my knees, as well as my spirit:

Worried about you, pal. You're in for a tough sled ahead if this doesn't go your way. Shaking it off won't be so easy. You may not pull through like you have before. It's actually frightening the more I think about it, so keep your fingers crossed. You're really up against it this time. Remember what Cagney said before he died in that rainy gutter. "I ain't so tough."

PLEASE, just give me the job and wash away these alien feelings.

"Congratulations," a hushed voice said, "you got the job," then quickly hung up.

It just so happened to be my next door neighbor who was set to be the 2nd A.D. on the film, and was right in the office when Robert Wise made his final casting choices. Mr. Wise hung up fourteen 8 x 10 pictures of his Sand Pebble crew, and one of them was me. I was absolutely ecstatic! My ship had come in. I could hardly wait for my agent to call. He never did.

Later, I learned what happened. As the casting person made deal after deal with twelve photos on the wall, Robert Wise returned from lunch and glanced at the two remaining 8 x 10's—mine and another actor. He studied them momentarily, then said the fateful words, "Do these two look alike?" My 2nd A.D. neighbor claimed he tried to help by saying, not really, but Mister Wise wasn't to be fooled. To be fair, he flipped a coin to see who he'd let go. It wasn't the other actor.

In the gambling world, the term 'bad beat' was always reserved for a loss that never should have happened, but did somehow. It twisted your insides in a way that felt personal and cruel. I never bought into the 'gods are against me' scenario, but losing a job in this manner was one painful blow. I felt kicked in the pit of the stomach. How could the simplicity of a coin flip carry such impact? My wife was great about it and said all the right things, but my mind wanted to shut down. No words were going to erase this feeling. I'd be back, but at that moment I just wanted to lie down and let it all drift away.

I Take It You Can Ride a Horse

While my career continued to languish in the toilet, I decided one day to call my latest agent and voice a minor complaint about not hearing from him since the day I'd signed six months earlier. He didn't miss a beat, and launched into how he had me up at that very moment for numerous important roles. Adding "Hang tight, Jerry. I'm not worried." It was time to find a new agent. My third. Hopefully, one who could remember my name.

Right off the bat, the 'aggressive' boutique agency I signed with next, landed me a two-part episode of the TV show, *Combat*. I was impressed with their speed, not the role. I played a sniveling coward and hated it, but was in no position to be choosy. So I 'sniveled' away as best I could. A mere five months later, I did an episode of *Gunsmoke*. Can't quite remember who or what I played, but I'm reasonably certain it wasn't Billy the Kid.

Another western show followed three months later. I was closing the gap between jobs, so that felt promising. This director didn't even ask me to read because he remembered me from my glory days in New York TV.

He just hit me with one question, "I take it you can ride a horse?"

"Like the wind," I said without hesitation. I'd been coached real well by other actors about this situation, and the key here was no hesitation. Full steam confidence puts you in the saddle. Any real riding went to the stunt people, so there was no need for worry.

Well for a few days my actor friends were dead on. All I was asked to do was just sit atop a horse and do a few lines of dialogue. No riding whatsoever. Pretty boring stuff, especially after having a ball before the shoot, riding rental horses. However, one day things finally picked up. I, along with my henchmen, were being asked to gallop past the camera in one scene. Terrific. We did it in one take. No problem. Felt like I was born in the saddle. Maybe the director felt the same way, because he decided to get creative and wanted me to do one more shot.

He wanted the cameraman to lie flat on his belly, and have me gallop within three yards short of him, make an abrupt stop...Give it the big think...Register determination...Then gallop on. This request put a small dent in my confidence. Galloping up to within three yards of the cameraman, after only two one-hour rides on a rented horse, gave me pause. Excellent chance I would trample the cameraman to death.

On the first take I made a fabulous abrupt stop. But—it was thirty-five yards shy of the mark. The director thought I misunderstood. Told me the abrupt stop looked great, but he wanted it to be THREE yards short of the camera. Huge close-up time, which felt like a favor being given due to our past history. I appreciated it, but expressed a trifle of concern about the camera man's safety. He said not to worry, the horse knows what he's doing. He's a professional. My only hope now was that the horse was such a pro, he would sense there was a lemon aboard, and it was up to him whether the camera man would live or die.

My next attempt came up fifteen yards short. The director told me to quit worrying about the camera man and just trust the horse to do its thing. Why did I say I rode like the wind?! If the poor bastard lying on his belly was a real man, he should have been peeing in his pants at this point. As the director yelled 'action' I went for broke. Hit the three-yard mark perfectly. One problem...It was three yards PAST the camera. Time to move on. Certainly, a letdown for actor and director, but a great moment for the camera man. He would live to shoot another day.

"No Chico, No Poker"

As for me, my career arc was still up for grabs. I figured to get some parts here and there, which would help in collecting unemployment, but other than that, making noise again in show business felt further away with every passing day. The role I seemed destined to play, whether I liked it or not, was 'every night poker player'. It was helping to pay the bills, but what a grind. So much so, that my wife felt I should take a day off.

"It's your birthday," she said. "We don't need the money that bad."

That wasn't true. I'd lost pretty good betting on sports that weekend and 'somehow' forgot to mention it. I needed to pay my bookie and had to at least try to make some money. Instead of giving her the real lowdown on the situation, I made up a story saying, 'I woke up feeling SO lucky, that if I turned my back on—'

"STOP," she cut me off. "You can play, but only under one condition." Which was, to go without argument to a hair stylist she had booked two months in advance as a surprise for my birthday. She had heard through the grapevine that he was a true artist, and that many actors saw their careers transformed overnight after getting a 'Chico' cut. It sounded like a bunch of crap to me, so when I began to stick up for my five dollar barber, she pointedly cut me off.

"No Chico, no poker."

I was off to see 'Mr. Magic Fingers'(his nickname). Chico had a fun personality, so things started off fine. How it ended was another story. He had a rule that forbade his customer to see what he was doing until his magic fingers completed their mission. The cut took so long I was barely awake when he finished.

Bursting with restraint, Chico led me to a mirror. "Don't you just love it?!" he erupted. Without waiting for an answer, Chico left the scene of the crime.

I was startlingly awake now. Staring at someone vaguely familiar. Within moments he returned with the gang. A chorus of 'chirpers' just as excited as Chico, oohing away at his heavenly creation. The consensus was I looked like Marlon Brando in *Julius Caesar* — only better. They particularly loved my bangs.

"Isn't he to die for," Chico squealed, erratically snipping away at the air, while jumping up and down.

Maybe my wife was on to something when she said Chico could transform one's career overnight. What's so bad with selling Hush Puppies for a living?

140

Come that evening, sporting Chico's artistry, plus a flowery denim outfit (another gift from the Mrs.), I was the comedy relief at the poker game. I was also the recipient of the worst run of luck I could remember. No matter what I was dealt, it wasn't good enough. I just couldn't get arrested.

Moments later, we were busted by the police.

Entrapment

Being jailed at the West Hollywood police station wasn't as bad as it might seem. Some of the players, being actors, were doing prison dialogue from old movies, and the cops were genuinely loving it. They even applauded at one point. Everybody seemed to be in high spirits. I took some credit for this, because it was probably a holdover from the laugh riot I created, thanks to Chico and the little woman.

After paying a small fine we were processed out, along with a kid who suggested we get the poker game going again. He had been heading for a Gardena poker club, but would rather play with us. It was still early evening, so after talking amongst ourselves, we agreed. For me, it was a no-brainer. It was a chance to win back some of my earlier losses.

We decided on someone's place, gave him the address, but didn't really expect him. To our surprise, he showed up an hour later. The kid sat next to me, but I could tell he was nervous. His hands were actually trembling a little. I attributed this to his young age and the strange surrounding, so I asked if he would feel more comfortable just to sit out a round and watch. He was very appreciative of my gesture and gratefully accepted. Halfway through the round though, he became more nervous, not less so. His hands were literally shaking uncontrollably, and I started to feel really sorry for this poor, innocent-looking kid.

Didn't last long though. Two deals later, a crashing axe came through the door and our young buck sprang to his feet, slammed the table with the palm of his hands, and yelled at the top of his quivering voice, "Don't anybody move. This is the police! You're under arrest!!"

Unbelievable!

Off we go to the slammer again, thanks to entrapment by a young cop planted in our cell, to specifically talk us into playing again. As the police car pulled away, I started to say something to a fellow arrestee, when a cop's nightstick instantly crammed the base of my throat.

When I voiced my protest over this aggressiveness, the creepy cop said, "Oh, will you listen to her."

That remark took me completely by surprise…till I remembered looking like a Roman peach. Now the Irish in me really came up. I was pissed at my wife, at Chico, and particularly this nasty bastard of a cop. As I let my feelings be known, his nightstick was jammed in deeper.

"Just wait till we get downtown, sweetie. We have a special place for your kind."

I was seething. The charm of the first bust a distant memory. We silently headed downtown to the Los Angeles City jail. After being booked and fingerprinted, we were put into a huge holding tank with about eighty other guys. From derelict to wino, to pimps, to petty thieves, it was a pretty depressing sight. ONE toilet bowl completely out in the open was to serve all. Most guys didn't ever bother, as they took pees and vomited in whatever corner they chose.

One huge black dude used the toilet bowl for the loudest crap I have ever heard. It was like this guy could take on the whole bean-eating crowd from the movie *Blazing Saddles*, and I would be betting on him. It was incredible. Disgustingly funny, but since NOBODY reacted or even looked his way, I too pretended to hear nothing. It was amazing, but in less than a moment, I was on my way to becoming a jailhouse pro. This was wise, because I really looked different from my fellow inmates, and was hoping to hell they wouldn't notice.

No such luck. Before long, a vicious little fight broke out between two guys standing right near me. I was darting back and forth to avoid an errant blow, which drew attention my way. Maybe it was paranoia, but I felt there were just as many eyes on me as there were

144

on the fight. I immediately switched my ballet athleticism into a more macho strut of indifference. I was working so hard on my performance, that when some flying blood from the fight landed on my face, I didn't even flinch. What's a little blood to a REALLY rough customer.

Thankfully, a few cops entered the tank and settled things down. I was only subjected to one more degrading incident. About an hour later, we were separated into groups of ten by the cops, and told to stand in a row, shoulder to shoulder. We did, and the cop said, "Anyone for de-licing step forward?"

I was immediately angered at what I perceived as a dehumanizing question. But in a flash, NINE GUYS stepped forward, leaving me standing alone. In an instant, it felt like my skin was crawling alive. When bail was finally posted, I went home and took a near scalding shower, hoping for a skin peel.

****

It wasn't long after that, my marriage ended. But I swear it had nothing to do with Chico. In fact, it was my wife who asked for the divorce. She still loved me she claimed, but this sort of life confused her and left her feeling unsettled. In truth, there was so much uncertainty surrounding my future, I certainly couldn't

145

blame her. Maybe a guy a little off center held some appeal in the beginning, but when it became apparent I had become a part-time actor and FULL-TIME GAMBLER, the thought of having kids, supplying food for the table, paying rent on time, was at best highly questionable.

Girls feel more comfortable when a husband has his feet planted firmly on the ground, and mine were admittedly a little shaky. Can you imagine if the roles were reversed, and your wife was betting the household money week after week on something you're not interested in? And even truly despise? Can you also imagine her losing the dough on a fairly regular basis.

—"Honey, you can't have steak this week because the Spartans of Michigan State went down the tubes on me."

—"Don't talk vacation to me, when I'm getting buried. You're lucky if I cook your fucking dinner tonight."

—"Stop for Christ's sake. There's no children until I make a real score. It's not your biological clock at stake."

I could go on but you get my gist. Our women deserve medals. Preferably made of diamonds, so that we can hock them in a pinch. If she's nutty enough to love

Tammy Wynette's recording of *Stand By Your Man*, then we got a chance. Other than that, fasten your seat belt, it's gonna be a bumpy ride.

Pigskin Guru

They say hindsight has 20-20 vision, but at the time, mine was clearly myopic. Maybe it was in the genes. My father was famous for betting on trotters that had a knack for 'galloping' at the wrong time; and my mother was convinced she was an incredible bingo player, despite results that seldom matched her confidence. Whatever the reasons, my career trajectory was heading down south at a steady clip, so being young and immortal required short-term memory. The prior New York experience of two strong- arm money collectors wanting to break something in my body, and surviving Roy's bowling alley, had already disappeared from mind.

I was gambling day and night, and more so on the weekends, wagering on football, trying to rediscover the unique ability I once had for picking winners. At the time, betting on the college and pro games was all the rage in the Hollywood community. Especially in the theatrical softball league I had joined. Even though I hadn't quite reached the football magic of my early New York days, I still had the touch. As my handicapping reputation grew, so did my friendship with a lot of the important show biz crowd. Many of whom were caught up in a sport they couldn't make payoff. So I became somewhat of a 'guru' that could change that.

One Hollywood big shot told me he was smart enough to realize what an idiot he was for losing his money and mind, year after year, but football ruled him. It was Kong in his jungle. Call it the 800 pound gorilla or Glenn Close in a monkey suit, it was a 'fatal attraction'. He was tortured over lack of CONSISTENCY! Stay goddamn consistent!! If a team was bad, he wanted them to remain bad. That, he considered a positive thing. He just didn't want them to play like crap one week, then like a world-beater the following. He was always getting caught in the switches. Lamenting that even when he was savvy enough to avoid the original trap, he then had to face the reverse trap—then the double reverse trap—and eventually the brain freeze. It was just too mind-boggling to handle. He sounded like my old pal, Danny Kaye in the *Court Jester:*

— I've got it! I've got it! The pellet with the poison's in the vessel with the pestle; the chalice from the palace has the brew that is true! Right?
— Right, but there's been a change. They broke the chalice from the palace.
— They broke the chalice from the palace?!
— And replaced it with a flagon.
— A flagon?
— With the figure of a dragon.
— Flagon with a dragon.
— Right.
— But did you put the pellet with the poison in the

vessel with the pestle?

— No! The pellet with the poison's in the flagon with the dragon! The vessel with the pestle has the brew that is true!

— The pellet with the poison's in the flagon with the dragon; the vessel with the pestle has the brew that is true.

— Just remember that.

(Panama/Frank, 1955 *The Court Jester*, Paramount Pictures)

Funny how entertaining poison can be. While gamblers build up immunity, bookmakers build up annuity. One of the unfortunate victims of wagering on football was a big time theatrical agent named Guy McElwaine. We met in the Entertainment Softball League and bonded over our football interests. Monday night football at McElwaine's house became a ritual.

A number of important, die-hard bettors were always in attendance. Directors, producers, movie moguls, agents, actors, athletes, you name it. Steven Spielberg, Alan Ladd Jr., Richard Brooks, Frank Wells, James Caan, OJ Simpson, Richard Pryor, etc. The list goes on and on. The conversation was lively and witty up to a point. But once the ball was in the air on the kickoff, it was down to serious business. The amounts bet on Monday night were always stupidly high. Guy would look to avoid all client calls. Except for one night.

Richard Dreyfuss called with a pressing problem. He was working on a movie called, *What About Bob,* and started telling Guy that Bill Murray, his co-star, had just deliberately thrown a chair at him, narrowly missing his head. At that moment, the team Guy was betting against, threw a seventy-two yard touchdown pass, and in sheer disgust, Guy yelled out, "Shit!"

I'm sure Dreyfuss felt that his agent had really gotten the urgency of Murray's attack on him, because moments later Guy said, "No, no, terrible, terrible," while pointing out the touchdown rerun in disgust. In Hollywood, being able to multitask, while being quick on your feet, is a must.

As for me, the demand on my opinion was pressure packed. I had to stay calm and centered. I knew if I let others (no matter how important they were) stoke my ego, I would be in big trouble. Being a 'feel' bettor, I needed to feel free to fail. And ego and freedom don't work well together.

Outside factors like weather conditions, home field advantage, day games, night games, match ups, injuries, smart money guys, etc., meant little to me. If I couldn't feel who the winner was, I wouldn't go near the game. I depended on my antenna to predict outcome, so I had to go into a private space within myself to access it. If I could reach a comfort level on a certain team, without any 'lingering' sense of fear, that would be the ticket for me.

To accomplish this, I would take a toke of weed, put myself into a hot tube, and 'feel out' the game. Whichever team came clear for me on an energetic level, that's who I would be betting on. My approach carried much humor for the Hollywood community, but they couldn't wait to find out what my selections would be. They would call each other to confirm that I had entered the tub, and if so, the word spread not to call me until I emerged. I have no idea why it worked as well as it did. Who knows, maybe outcome was in the airways and I was getting a sneak preview of it.

Whatever the reason, I was picking more winners than anyone else, and that's all that mattered to my new found, big-betting friends. They couldn't care if I wanted to hang feet first from a Bodhi Tree, as long as it produced the results they wanted. For this crowd, 'real money' was changing hands based on my opinion.

Before, I could privately lick my wounds if I lost. Now, I had everybody else's wounds to deal with. Disappointing yourself is one thing, but disappointing others entices your ego to enter the fray. Now I had to spend time telling my ego if I lost, I lost. Didn't make me a bad person. My selection might suck, but so what and who cares. Ego, of course, wasn't buying any of it.

152

It knew how to confront vulnerability. It was a master at it. The message it peddled was: *Stop kidding yourself. You've been chasing a sense of importance for some time. Don't blow it now. You've gotta come through here. The stakes are too high.*

Soon as the fear factor entered, my ability to produce winners took a hit. I wasn't bailing out peoples' hopes and dreams at the rate they wanted, and the grumbling started. Not from the bookies, mind you, who were greatly relieved because they were getting killed from the Hollywood bettors, thanks to me. But when the script didn't go as intended, many of the Hollywood crowd turned to gripe mode.

"I would have had the winner of that game. Why did I ever listen to that guy."

It didn't come as a surprise to me, but still, it was a turnoff. People who were recently clamoring to be in my orbit, now disappeared. Suddenly, I was yesterday's news again. I had been down that road before. First as a child star, now as a football guru.

I told myself from now on I would keep my opinion to myself. Forget the fanfare. It's not worth the extra credit. Just get the job done and be satisfied with that.

Easy enough to say, but ego likes 'special', so I would have to keep my guard up.

Freeze Frame Moment

'Getting healthy' for most people means proper diet, exercise, good rest, vitamins, etc. For me, it meant playing winning poker, and covering the spread on a regular basis. A real tough proposition under any circumstance, but adding drugs to it would be fatal. I had to stay razor sharp to survive. No easy task, because this was the height of the drug culture. Grass and cocaine were an everyday occasion.

I wasn't into any judgement about these items, I just couldn't afford the luxury of being spaced out too often. As for cocaine, there was absolutely no stigma attached to it at the time. It was on the menu, morning, noon, and night. What saved me there was it just made my nose run off my face. Couldn't handle it at all. Which made for a singular occurrence.

One late afternoon, I was walking with my friend Elliott, who's now at a place where the last name of Gould means a lot more than when he first stepped off the elevator at Professional Children's School, dressed as a Frog Man. Snorkel, mask, spear gun, the whole deal. In his defense it was April Fools Day. But when one thinks of a movie star…he wasn't it. Throw in James Dean and Nicholson that made me 0-3, when it came to picking future movie stars. If you're an actor, you better hope I don't think you're going very far. Becoming a movie star definitely added to Elliott's confidence. Stopping in front of a private club on the Sunset Strip called ON THE ROX, Elliott asked if I wanted to go up and see it. He wasn't a member, but said let's ring the bell and see what happens. He did. Someone said hello. The moment Elliott gave his name, the buzzer responded instantly. Name value unlocks a lot of doors in Hollywood.

We went up one flight to a club that was so dark, I wasn't sure we'd get a drink or be mugged. It took a while for our eyes to adjust to the fact that the club was empty, except for a man and woman talking in hushed tones. Turned out to be Ryan O'Neal, a big star at the time, and Sue Mengers, hot shot agent of big stars. We sat down. Somebody, that filled in as a shadow, brought us a drink, then disappeared into the void. It felt that if I spoke above a whisper, Elliott would lose his chance to pay some silly amount to become a member of this tomb, so mum was the word…until Elliott suggested we head for the bathroom and do a line of 'coke'.

At that moment, despite my adverse reaction to cocaine, it felt like a pretty good idea. Off we went, ever so slowly, because stupid us forgot to bring our flashlights. As we were about to do our 'line', in walks Ryan O'Neal. Elliott, always polite and generous,

156

asked Ryan if he would like to join us in a toot. Without hesitation Ryan joyfully accepted, and upon completion, reached into his waist band for his vial of cocaine to offer a snort in return.

As we were indulging, in walked Ringo Starr. Naturally Elliott and Ryan asked Ringo if he would like to join in.

"Absolutely," said Ringo.

After a healthy snort, he reached down into his sock and offered up his stash. Runny nose be damned. This was history in the making and I wasn't going to be a spoil sport. Besides being a freeze frame moment, I can even recall the quality of the merchandise. Elliott's coke was perfectly fine. Ryan's rose above perfectly fine to be a real sinus opener. And Ringo's reached across all party lines to other worldly. Talk about blowing everyone's socks off! My god!!

Truly, This Man Was the Son of God

Fifty-five hours later, when my cocaine nose was down to a minor drip, I was back to playing cards, and learned that God had shed his grace on two of my poker buddies. Butch and Dick Bakalyan had been cast in George Stevens' epic Christ movie, *The Greatest Story Ever Told*. They would be playing the good and bad thief on the cross, sandwiching Max Von Sydow in the role of Jesus Christ. The shoot was suppose to go on forever, so I was naturally a bit envious.

On the positive side, I knew they would have fresh money. And since I was the better poker player, maybe this was God's way I could share in their wealth without the discomfort of being nailed to a cross. I'd heard God worked in mysterious ways, and since he chose to make me a mystery in show business, maybe He could make it up with a heart-filled winning flush. It didn't play out quite that way. Maybe by making that movie, the heavenly spirit had enlightened Butch, because he was playing inspired poker. It wasn't that I was losing; I just wasn't filling the coffers as much, that's for sure—EXCEPT for one priceless story:

Every day, Butch would tell me horror stories about director Stevens unmerciful putdowns of cast and crew. An out-and-out killer on the set. I hated to hear that because Stevens directed *Gunga Din*, one of my favorite movies of all time. Butch relished in telling each putdown story of the day—Until it was his turn in the barrel. In the big crucification scene, with rain driving wildly, Stevens yelled cut and started lambasting Butch.

"You up there, why are you fluttering your eyelids? You were hired to play the bad thief, but somehow think you're the Virgin Mary. Will someone please inform that asinine person up there fluttering his eyelids, that he is not the VIRGIN MARY."

Butch said it went on like that until Stevens ran out of breath. There was literally only one person spared from Stevens' wrathful tongue lashing, and that was Marion Robert Morrison (AKA), John Wayne.

Big 'Duke' was a legendary cowboy movie star, and considered Hollywood Royalty. He'd been hired by Stevens to play the main Roman Centurion, who had only one line. BUT IT WAS THE KEY LINE. The moment Christ dies, the sky opens up in serious outrage. Howling winds, driving rain, furious lightening strikes, the works! A scene which cries out for 'one' take because of the massive time delay in setting up to go again. So the big moment comes. Jesus dies and every special effect goes crazy wild! Wayne, after witnessing heaven's major upset, steps forward, looks up at Jesus and drawls—"Truly, this man was the son of Gawd"...Profound silence. As Butch recounts, the line is said as only you can imagine cowpoke Wayne delivering it, with the same inflection Big John used in every western he's ever done. Stevens, eventually finding his voice, says simply..."Let's go again."

Three hours later, the berserk crazy effects accompany Wayne's EXACT SAME LINE READING! Another huge silence ensues.

Stevens then says with gentle reverence, "Let's try this again, shall we?"

Two more failures later with absolutely no change, Butch, still dangling on the cross, overhears Stevens say to Wayne, "You know what I think is missing, Duke...It's awe. I really believe awe is the key."

Wayne loves it! Nods vigorously. "Gotcha, Pappy."

Many weary hours later the big scene arrives once again. Christ dies. The skies open up. Wayne now steps forward with supreme confidence and says—"Awww...truly, this man was the son of Gawd..."

Now that might not be the Greatest Story ever told, but it runs a close second. Even writing about it today makes me laugh.

No Can of Corn

Extracting humor from most situations was a saving grace for me. It didn't take a mental giant to realize a gambler's life was no can of corn. Trying to remain a winner in a loser's game was quite a magic trick. Everyday I was under fire from some forward pass, three point shot, line drive, busted hand, photo finish, Dad's phone calls, etc. Part of you always feels you're in the bottom of the ninth praying for a comeback, while the poorhouse whispers 'don't forget about me.' Always trying to undermine confidence and have me question myself. 'Still under the spell of believing you're in control of things, hotshot?'

I knew the answer to that, but had no space for peril chatter. Swimming upstream was hard enough. Salmon was written all over me as I struggled to reach the promise land before the bear ate me. Who knows, maybe I 'needed' the odds stacked against me to perk my interest. To make the game more exciting. Electrical currents abounding, charged and ready for action. Dr. Frankenstein yelling, "He's alive! He's alive!" You get the picture. Arms outstretched, trudging forward, looking like shit, waiting for the bride to reject me.
Well BARRIERS BE DAMNED! Perseverance is not a word for me. It's a religion. Tapping out was just a small bump in the road. I knew I was moving too fast for my

own good, but that's the nature of the beast. I'm sure all the ups and downs were taking a toll on my adrenal system, but as long as I was managing to pay the bills, it had my undivided attention. Acting and gambling were all I ever knew, and neither one had any security attached to it. So being able to shake off all negatives was an element of survival. Not easy when control was slipping away, and compulsiveness is on your tail and picking up speed.

Every losing football game, poker hand, audition, was doing it's best to crumble my confidence. I had to hold onto that, or the game would be over. Throwing in the towel was not an option. I was used to handling disappointment, so why not stay positive about my chances of success.

One night though, after a losing poker session, I was having trouble shaking off the loss. I'd played like an idiot, and my mind decided to step in and read me the riot act. It was after me big time. 'What the hell is wrong with you? Who gave you the luxury of letting up? Your life is skating on thin ice, don't you get that? You're lucky I'm still concerned or I wouldn't even waste good breath on you. Shape up, for god's sake! Get fucking serious!'…It was doing it's best to convince me I was doing life all wrong.

On top of this dour head space, there was a guy on the radio named 'Deathpool Demitri,' expounding on how much he depended on inside information for his winning results. He went on to talk about how his friends, bet their bookie, on celebrities that will die within a twelve month period. For instance, he received word about a certain rock group guy who was into hard drugs, and bet he wouldn't make it past a year.

The rocker OD'd, and Deathpool Demitri said he picked up a nice piece of change. He also made out like a bandit on Gene Siskel, the noted movie critic of Siskel and Ebert fame. After hearing from a hospital informant that they removed a tumor the size of a golf ball from Mr. Siskel's head, he quickly bet thumbs down against the movie critic. Shortly thereafter, Gene didn't disappoint him.

But the sweetest score ever made, he said, was on the demise of John Kennedy, Jr. Based on inside information that the plane John purchased was a little too sophisticated for a novice pilot, he took 125 to 1 for fifty bucks that Kennedy Jr. wouldn't make it through one year. On this fatal event, old Deathpool Dimitri said, and I quote, "He came through for me big time. His swan dive was worth 6,250."

Listening to this was a reality check. I knew that gambling could be a rough business, but Deadpool Dimitri took it to another dimension. I made myself a promise right then and there, that if a 'kicker' missed a short, spread-covering field goal that had me wanting his leg amputated, I would check myself immediately into rehab. I'm not proud to say I had to bite my tongue on a few occasions. Whatever happened to that sweet little boy from *Hans Christian Andersen*?

Fessing Up

This feels like the moment to fess up to my own inside information. Around this time I got a call from Elliott, telling me that the late Jack Kent Cooke had invited him and a guest to have dinner and watch his L.A. Lakers play basketball. Naturally I'm up for that. At this point in time, being a big star, gambling on sports for Elliott had reached the 'what for' level. But for me, it was a necessity. So I bet a thousand bucks on the game, split it with Elliott, and we're off to see Mr. Cooke.

We were met at the Forum by his right hand man, a guy sporting an ill-fitting brown suit, brown shirt, black tie, bad hat, and the personality of a clam. In stone silence he led us to Jack Kent Cooke's office. As we entered his rather large office, Mr. Cooke was on the telephone, but smiled and indicated to us to come forward. He was talking to the owner of the St. Louis Hawks, and the conversation went like this… "You think you've got problems (laughs)…This team is going to slaughter us. Besides being riddled with injuries, I just got a call from the dressing room a minute ago that my two stars Elgin Baylor and Jerry West won't be able to play. I might have to suit up. (Laughs) Can you imagine playing our entire bench against these fellows?"

Well, I could imagine. I glanced over at Elliott like someone had just picked my pocket for 500 bucks. The only reason I bet this dumb thing was because of the invite and to have a rooting interest. I certainly wasn't crazy about our action because the Lakers were going against the all-powerful Milwaukee Bucks who, led by Lew Alcindor (Kareem Abdul-Jabbar), were busy breaking records, steamrolling through all of the NBA competition. Not only do we have a horrible losing bet, but we also have powerful info the gambling world does not know yet. Juicy stuff.

My mind was crazed as I looked around and spotted a telephone in the far end of his office. Do I dare? The answer is—yes, of course. Maybe it was just paranoia, but as I looked toward the 'clam,' he's staring at me like he knows what I'm about to do. It startles me momentarily, but I whisper to Elliott to keep him busy while I use the phone to call my bookie. Elliott's expression turns to concerned horror, but I'm already on my way. When I pick up the phone and start to dial, Elliott moves forward to engage the clam. What a team.

The phone is busy of course, and as I keep redialing, the pressure mounts. Finally I get through, but naturally I'm forced to whisper. I keep giving him my code number and identification, and he keeps telling me to speak up, he can't hear a word I'm saying. I nervously glance over toward Elliott and see the henchman looking more at me than listening to Elliott. Finally, I raise my volume just enough so he can make out what I'm saying, but nobody else. Here I am trying to get down for a two thousand dollar bet, which is my limit at the time, and the bookmaker is still telling me to speak up...or he's going to hang up.

In panic, I blurted out that I wanted two thousand on Milwaukee over the Lakers. I can't believe how loud I said it. My heart stopped beating for a moment.

"Can you repeat that", the bookie asked.

"No!" I said adamantly. "You heard me the first time."

There was a beat.

"You want two dimes on Milwaukee -4 over the Lakers?"

"Yes."

"You got it," my bookie replied, "but what's with the feather up your ass?"

I apologized for my rudeness, lied about having had a root canal that day, and mercifully ended the conversation. At that moment, I heard Jack Kent Cooke hang up. I was afraid to turn because I felt everybody heard everything. Then Cooke says in the most chipper of voices, "Elliott Gould, how are you?!"

As I turned, he was all smiles. Elliott introduced me, and I told him I had an emergency call to make and hoped he didn't mind me using his phone. He said not at all, still beaming from ear to ear. The clam however, just glared at me.

We had a lovely dinner with Mr. Cooke, who all through the game, kept apologizing for how badly his Lakers were performing. Being two actors, we commiserated quite convincingly, while secretly enjoying his 39 point defeat. We lost $1100 to one bookmaker and beat the other for $2000. A total win of $900.

Many years after, Elliott and I had decided to tell Mr. Cooke what we had done because he had a good sense of humor. But he left L.A. when he bought the Washington Redskins and we never got around to talking to him before he died.

Anyway, sorry for the indiscretion, Mr. C...I just couldn't help myself at the time.

Divine Intervention

The constant struggle to keep my head above water was wearing me down, but it was what it was. No crying the blues. That was not so for Dad. He was always in abject misery over my nonexistent career, and never tired of telling me about it. His constant badgering had to be stopped, but how? Couldn't hit him with 'appointment with adventure' again, so I said simply, "You know, Pa, you're right." Told him that everything he was saying was making a whole lot of sense, and with a very assuring tone, stated, "I'll start Monday." For some reason that halted him from pressing forward with his slam fest. A little win for some people, but to me it was like making a major score. Maybe things were on the upswing.

Bumping into Edward Dmytryk, the man who directed me in *The Juggler* when I was a kid, felt like divine intervention. I was on my way to an eye exam (needed more distant vision), when I spot a shiny, heads-up penny. It's newness glittered in the sunlight as I passed. I took two more steps, then stopped cold. Good Luck? Who knows? Turn back? Why not? Despite almost knocking Dmytryk down, he was delighted to see me, and in no hurry to leave. Wanting to know everything, especially in terms of my career, I told him the truth.

He informed me that he would soon be directing a war movie in Italy called *Anzio*, and would see if he could get me in it. He couldn't promise anything until he deals with Dino De Laurentiis (the producer) because they still had to negotiate requests and favors. A give and take sort of thing.

The whole conversation felt so honest, that I left with a bounce in my step. Did the universe intercede on my behalf, knowing I needed something, anything, that would give me relief from the pressures of Dad and the gambling grind? Kinda felt like that. But after months passed without a word, it had already left my mind.

I don't remember the exact day my agent called, but let's call it Monday just because. He was quite excited to tell me how he landed me a job in a big war movie called *Anzio*, to be filmed in Italy. Must have been quite an effort on my agent's part to pull this baby off, but I was happy enough to spare him any further commentary.

Anzio

Three months in Italy, playing one of seven American soldiers trapped behind enemy lines, was a godsend. Although I must admit, it didn't start very well. In fact, it was down right scary. Peter Falk, who I'd worked with in early New York TV and knew well, had recently become a rising movie star. Upon completing his latest film, Falk arrived in Italy one week later than the rest of the cast. He hadn't even had time to read the script, and wanted to know what I thought about it. I gave him my honest opinion, which was, 'not very good'. No problem for me. I was just grateful to have the job. An innocent comment between friends, right? Wrong.

Next morning, the Assistant Director arrived with startling news. The day's shoot had been canceled, and possibly the whole picture. He proceeded to tell me that Peter Falk heard from 'someone' that the script was a turkey. He'd read it, agreed wholeheartedly, and was quitting the picture. UN..FUCKING BELIEVABLE!

Clearly knowing who that 'someone' was, I prayed that Falk hadn't named names. The irony being director, Edward Dmytryk, was treated harshly for naming names during the Joseph McCarthy communist witch hunt. The dread I felt was warranted. My name value was already on life support, so pulling the plug on me would be a piece of cake. Just fade to black and get it over with. As it happened, Falk never squealed on me, and worked out an agreement with De Laurentiis. Close down the picture for one week, allow Peter to rewrite his part, and he would stay.

After that near debacle, things settled down and shooting a movie in Rome felt like a dream scenario. Until one day I had a rude awakening. Sitting outside the Cafe de Paris (a once famous tourist destination on the Via Veneto), I saw a number of wealthy Arabs, dressed resplendently in white tunics, seemingly everywhere. Hadn't a clue what this was all about. Maybe they were making Lawrence of Arabia II, who knew? When I inquired about it, my waiter said in a derisive manner, that the rich always get out of town when the going gets rough. He went on to explain that all hell had broken loose. A number of Arab countries teamed up to attack Israel, and they were being swarmed from all sides.

My mind instantly tracked back to 1952 when I first landed in Israel to film The Juggler. I was fifteen years old then, and now fifteen years later, Israel is being attacked by the Arabs again? This was difficult to get my head around. Here I was performing 'make believe' once again, this time playacting war, while the Israelis were at it for real, fighting for their lives. Of course, Yael Dayan came to mind, and I hoped she wouldn't get herself killed. I knew her to be strong and determined, as well as her people, but from what I was hearing, the odds were definitely not on their side.

Looking around at everyone enjoying themselves with food and drink, my mind was engaged in a battle all its own. It was torn between the life and death struggle going on in Israel, and the bad news my waiter had just delivered. They may have run out of Almond Croissant, my favorite. Shouldn't Israel's dire situation have wiped the croissant from my mind? Didn't I care enough about what was truly important? People are fighting and dying; forget about the friggin' almond croissant. This certainly didn't feel like my finest moment. If I ever met Yael again, would I own up to this story?

I was lost in that thought when the very last Almond Croissant arrived, looking better than ever. The waiter was beyond pleased he'd come through for me, since it was meant for an Arab sheik when he stole it. As he said, a firing situation if management found out. Now what was I supposed to do? Tell him I didn't want it due to some guilt trip over Israel. It was bad enough that I was now forced into a bigger tip, so why don't I just suck it up and eat the goddamn croissant.

At that moment, another waiter approached my guy and began quarreling in Italian. I assumed it was about the stolen croissant, and I was right. When I handed the plate back to the angry waiter, he thanked me profusely, while still leaving pissed off at his co-worker. This in turn had my waiter leave, pissed off at me. Didn't matter. I had taken my soul off the hook. Not to suggest that if I failed here I would live in infamy for the rest of my life, but still, I felt pretty good that my character wasn't totally toppled by a lowly croissant. Six days later, I felt even better when the Israelis had beaten the odds and had wiped out the formidable forces stacked against them.

Robert Mitchum

Meanwhile, back in my 'movie war', there was little excitement to be found. It's not unusual to have long stretches of waiting around, doing nothing on movie sets. So when someone (I'm innocent this time) suggested starting up a poker game, I thought it was a splendid idea and accepted without hesitation. Robert Mitchum, the star of the picture, didn't play, but often watched.

One day, he strode over to me and said, "Young man, I've been watching you play poker and you are double tough. Let's have a drink tonight after the shoot."

We did. That led to us becoming inseparable for the rest of the movie. He just seemed to adopt me. Never quite understood it, but didn't care. He was the best storyteller I ever met, and brought to life the characters he was talking about with pitch perfect accents. From his early days on a southern chain gang, to colorful and racy movie star stories that are much too intimate to tell even now. Although, there's one story I can relate which will give you a flavor of Mitchum.

Through the course of our conversations, Bob learned I was a 'big fan' of Ava Gardner, so he told me that he and Ava were close friends. She loved to stir up trouble, he said, and was always trying to bed him down. Broke my heart when he said no matter how hard she persisted, he never gave in. How can you not go to bed with Ava Gardner?! I couldn't believe him. I refused to. He said it was the truth, and since he spoke of so many wild affairs with other female stars, there was actually no reason not to believe him. He loved Ava as a wild and crazy friend, and that was it.

So a night arrives when Mitchum is dining at one of Hollywood's fancy restaurants, when Ava spots him, walks over, and 'hits' on him for later. Mitchum passes. Ava, now pissed, walks back to her table where she's sitting with three mobsters. Minutes later, one of the mobsters approaches Mitchum real menacingly. "We asked Ava to have you come over and join us for a drink, and she said, you said, 'I don't drink with greasy guinea mobsters'."

Mitchum calmly replied, "That's just Ava looking to start trouble, and if you believe a word she says, you're a bigger idiot than you look like. But if the truth is not good enough for you, we can take this outside and settle it right now."

The mobster didn't take up Mitchum's offer. I asked if he got mad at Ava for doing such a dangerous thing. He shrugged, "No, of course not. She was having some fun. Just Ava being Ava."

Being with Mitchum was like palling around with a character I've seen in all his movies. I never once saw him outwardly rattled. Talk about having an 'even keel' approach. The thought of him having a shouting match or a temper tantrum was unimaginable. Mitchum never seemed to have any need to act out emotions, both on and off screen. Even when I experienced upset in him, it came in a simple manner.

There's a scene in *Anzio* where we have to run down a steep ravine, and the camera is literally a half-mile away, shooting from a mountaintop. There was no way you could make out anything but distant figures, heading down the ravine. So I asked Mitchum why aren't they asking your stand-in to do this. Mitchum simply said, "Because they're stupid."

"Yeah," I said, "but shouldn't you tell them?" It wasn't his job, he replied. If he breaks his leg, which causes them to shut the movie down, it'll serve them right. It was that simple for Bob.

Getting busted for marijuana possession right after he became a movie star, made front page headlines all over the world. During that time, something like that would have been a sure career-destroyer. Yet Mitchum told me it made him more in demand. Enhanced his image. Fit the public's perception of him to a tee. For me, that unintended development would be like dodging a bullet. For Mitchum, he couldn't care less which way it went down. Up to that point in my life, if anyone else said something like that, I wouldn't have believed them. Yet coming from Mitchum, there was no doubt I heard the truth. He was that kind of authentic.

Yet there was one incident with Mitchum I never understood until writing this piece, and even now I can't be totally certain. There's one scene in *Anzio* where we had no other choice but to run across a mine field, hoping to survive. Mitchum first, me second, Falk third. Moments before Dmytryk is about to yell action, Mitchum leans across me and says to Falk, "Do you eat mice?"

Right on cue, action is called and we make our death defying dash.

For the rest of the day, Peter never stops muttering to me about Mitchum's remark. "Do I eat mice…Do I eat mice…What the hell does that mean? The guy has never said a word to me, not even a hello, and then asks me, do I eat mice. What the fuck?"

Picture for a moment how those words would tumble out of Falk's mouth, and you can see how you couldn't help but laugh. Basically I told him it was an odd statement, had no idea what he meant, and just ask him. Peter never did, nor did I. According to Peter, for the rest of the movie, not another word was ever

178

spoken between Mitchum and him. Well, after all these years, I might have solved the mystery. And if right, (something we will never know) it feels rather obvious. Here's my theory: At the time of the movie, Mitchum is an established movie star, and Falk is just up and coming. Yet it's Falk that has the movie shut down in the beginning to rewrite his part. Think of how Mitchum must have accepted that? I wouldn't think very well. So when Mitchum said to Falk, "Do you eat mice," just maybe it was Mitchum's way of telling Falk he's a 'snake'. Like I said, we'll never know for sure, so your guess will be as good as mine. Mitchum being Mitchum?

A postscript to the Ava story: After *Anzio* wrapped, Mitchum was heading off to Spain and told me if I wanted to come, he would introduce me to Ava. I took him up on his offer. When I arrived at Mitchum's hotel, low and behold in walks Ava! I assumed she was coming to see Bob, but it wasn't the case. It was just a coincidence. When he tried to reach her, she had already left and I never did get to meet her. So close, but it wasn't to be.

Looking back on the *Anzio* experience, there is one last story to tell. While on location in a small town call Taranto, I'm assigned to share a dressing room with a young Italian actor. Unfortunately for me, he was super intent on mastering the English language.

All day long he kept repeating, "Giancarlo is sitting on the sofa. The sofa is where Giancarlo is sitting."

The incessant refrain strained my feeling toward a really nice kid, who I liked a lot. So I just gagged myself and said nothing. That's over now. It's pay back time. Why do I say that? Well, since *Anzio*, not only have you, Giancarlo Giannini, risen to the point of being called the Second Coming to screen legend Marcello Mastroianni, you've also become the official Italian 'dubber' of Al Pacino, plus dubbing my old buddy, Jack Nicholson's voice in *The Shining* and *Batman*.

Giancarlo, if you're reading this, try to remember who your guinea pig was on *Anzio*. The one who endured your quest to master the English language on your rise to fame and fortune.

'Giancarlo is sitting on a pile of lira—A pile of lira is where Giancarlo is sitting.' Repeat. Repeat.

'Dear Giancarlo, I do think a mental-stress gift of any kind would travel a long way toward making amends. Love, Joseph Walsh'

Jack Lemmon and His Just Desserts

Back in Hollywood, it was same old, except for Mitchum. He had made sure we traded phone numbers, but I didn't plan to call. Why bother the guy? He was nice enough on the movie set, but this was real life. What did I have to offer Robert Mitchum? He didn't need me, and God forbid somebody would think I was using him. Definitely a shortcoming on my part that made me feel I was doing the right thing. It's funny what you protect in life due to your own shyness and sense of image.

Bob Mitchum had no such problem. He called within a week of my return. Couldn't wait for me to be part of his special New Years Eve party, where he would cook his famous midnight black-eyed pea dinner for just a few of his oldest and dearest friends. I was being invited into his inner circle and it was hard to understand. For Bob, it was so less confusing. He considered me a friend. Nothing more. Nothing less.

The evening was perfect Mitchum. Not a pretense to be found. Laid-back with good humor, and faces that had starred or had been featured in movies of the late forties and beyond. It was like being transported back to 'old Hollywood', and I was being accepted as one of them. It felt pretty special. It's not everyday you're handed a whole new wonderful family. Everyone seemed liked a gifted storyteller, but Mitchum excelled. Even though Jack Lemmon wasn't there that evening, Mitchum didn't spare his close friend from being the headliner of one of his favorite stories.

Once a month, Mitchum and his wife, Dorothy, would have dinner in an expensive Hollywood restaurant, along with five other couples. Lemmon and his wife being one of them. After about two and a half years, someone in the group noticed that Lemmon had the uncanny ability of leaving for the bathroom just before the check arrived. Upon reflection, the guys all came to the conclusion that he had never picked up one single check in all that time.

So Mitchum decided on a plan that was accepted with gleeful delight by the others. They would all leave for the bathroom simultaneously and once gone, the waiter would deliver the dinner check to Lemmon. Part of the plan was to really live it up that night, with extra bottles of really good champagne.

As the guys were in the bathroom, fully enjoying Lemmon's predicament, the only lament they had was not being able to see his face when he was handed the really expensive tab. Dorothy made their day by literally swearing that Jack's pallor went so pale, she thought he was a chameleon.

The ironic part to the story, which I didn't share with the group, was that as a kid I co-starred with Lemmon on live television. He played a highly likable guy who was secretly out to kill me. Can't remember why, but I'm sure it wasn't for exposing him as a check dodger.

Playing Poker with John Huston

As fun as that evening was, I knew I couldn't afford to get too attached. These people's lives were set, and I was scrambling to survive. I had to make money to stay afloat. Mitchum always said if I was up for anything, or knew about a certain part in a movie, to call him. If he knew someone involved, he'd be more than happy to put in a big plug for me. He really wanted to help in that way, but I knew I'd never call him for things like that. In fact, because of survival needs I let our relationship drift away to a point of where it was no more. No matter the circumstances, it doesn't feel good when you can't find space for a friend.

While I was busy getting very few job offers, my phone kept ringing with plenty of poker offers. Poker was like a circuit. If you played in one game, you're invited to another. It seemed like everybody needed an extra player for their game. They didn't care if you were good or bad. They just needed an extra body. This led to a poker invite at the house of famed director, John Houston.

At the time, Mr. Huston was struggling with Emphysema and kept an oxygen tank at his ready, but his demeanor fought against anybody feeling sorry for him. He was joyful, elegant, competitive, and when he spoke, there was sheer poetry in the richness of the tone. It felt like I was watching a most enjoyable movie in which a poker game was being played.

The only thing he couldn't hide was the 'rattle' of his cough, which occurred every so often, bringing back the sad reminder that the end wasn't far off. Yet his spirit and love of the game of poker would immediately bounce back with vigor. He wouldn't allow time for anyone to slump into sorrow. His humor was always on display. On his five trips to the alter, he called it a mixed bag. Marrying a schoolgirl, a gentle woman, a motion picture actress, a ballerina, and a crocodile. Constant deposits to my memory bank.

As for the poker, he was a fierce competitor, out to win. So after weeks of playing with him, I noticed a certain play that he always used to ensure a successful outcome. Briefly stated: Five card stud is a game in which you get four open cards and one hole card. The rule is don't bet into an open pair unless you're looking for trouble, or have a plan. I was convinced Mr. Houston was too intelligent not to have a plan. His thinking was—if an open pair checked—and he had a higher pair, he would bet into him and pick up the easy dough. If by chance the checker re-raised him, he would fold, thereby never paying the penalty of his aggressive play. He was just playing the percentage.

Get as much out of the cards as you can, and when finally caught, high tail it out.

So when the situation arrived with me, I checked my open pair of fours. His hole card made him better than my fours, so he bet. I made a substantial re-raise and he immediately folded. It was no surprise. I felt very strongly that would be the result of how this played out. What happened next is why I'm relating the story. After two hours of play, we always broke for lunch, then played for two more hours.

So as I'm eating my lunch, Mr. Houston pulls up a chair next to me and quietly says, "Do you mind, son, if I ask you a question, and it's perfectly fine if you don't answer it?"

"Of course," I say, "what is it?"

He reiterates that he would have no problem if I didn't want to answer the question. I'm curious now what the question will be, and tell him he can ask me anything, and if I know the answer I'll certainly tell him. So he starts, and I'll put it in his words—at least as close as I can recall.

"Remember that hand we played about a half-hour ago, when you checked, I bet out and you re-raised?"

I told him I did.

186

"It's okay now…perfectly okay if you don't want to answer," he says for the third time, "but did you have more than that pair of fours?"

"No," I replied simply. "Just the fours."
At that moment, the man's face lit up in total admiration. He patted my knee enthusiastically.

"Well done, son…Well done!!" he declared jubilantly.

It's as if he were so proud of me, he couldn't contain himself. Amazing! Every player I ever encountered (including myself), who's ever been bluffed out of a pot, took some hit to their ego. With Mr. Houston, there wasn't even a tinge of ego involved. It was the purest moment I ever witnessed.

As I drove home that day, my number one priority, which was playing winning poker, didn't hold center stage. Highly unusual. Mr. Houston, by just being him, had altered that. In terms of life, he had upped the ante. Thoughts of who I was and where I was going, were getting harder to ignore. Mitchum, Houston, and even Gregory Peck had shown me elements of character to admire. If there was a higher game being played, it would have to wait. I had to fend for myself and wasn't ready for doing things any other way.

Besides, living on the edge was just part of my nature. And since gambling excited me in a way that kept me moving forward, that was good enough for now. I liked life and all it's adventures. Just like the night I caught a glimpse of what it could 'look and feel like' to be a gigantic star.

Elvis

Elvis Presley was doing a show in Vegas and Elliott asked me if I had ever seen him perform in person. I hadn't, nor had he. So Elliott suggested we go see him. Well, Mr. Presley did not shortchange his audience. Sweating profusely, he was giving his all and more. At one point during his show, he handed out beautiful silk handkerchiefs to whichever woman wanted them.

So many women lined up to receive one, I thought this could take forever. It did. But it was so mesmerizing to watch I couldn't take my eyes off it. Each hankie Presley presented, came with the most intimate, tender lip kiss imaginable. It felt like Presley, the ladies, and the audience were sharing a swoon-like moment. It was extraordinary. I didn't care if he sang another song. Keep the kissing going. It was a showstopper. When Presley finally did conclude his act, Elliott wanted to go back and say hello to him. He didn't know Presley, but he was Elliott Gould at this point, so why not.

As we approached his dressing room, his black-belt bodyguard/friend, Red West, was coming out. To understand why this is newsworthy, let's fade back to the Hollywood softball league. Not only was it enjoyable to play in, but as the James Garner story can attest, highly competitive. Show biz people REALLY like to win.

As I was sliding into home plate one game, the catcher slams the ball into my face. A TAGOUT IN THE FACE! Well, now I'm really pissed and let this guy know it. He calmly responded, if you got a problem, pal, we can take it up right after the ballgame. In my upset I instantly told him, let's do that. Bad move.

"The guy you're about to encounter is Red West," said Butch, my teammate. "A total killer, and protector of Elvis Presley."

Gulp. My bruised face was soon to be rearranged after the final out. I remained outwardly defiant, but secretly hoped the ball game would go into extra innings. Say about forty-seven, when it would be so dark he'd never find me. No such luck. The game was over shortly thereafter. As I removed my spikes, I saw Red heading right toward me, and immediately put on my best tough guy face. Just as he reaches me, I stand. At which point he sticks out his hand to shake, while apologizing profusely for the horrible tag to my face. It didn't take me long to forgive him. What's a little crushed face between friends.

The same Red West, coming out of Presley's dressing room, seemed more than happy to see us, treating me

190

like a long lost friend. I told him that Elliott and I just stopped by to say hello to Elvis. Great, says Red, and as he opens the dressing room door, I immediately spot Elvis starting to button this fabulous velvet blue jacket.

Elliott sees something else. "Elvis, open your jacket. I saw it."

I had no idea why Elliott was saying such a thing, but Elvis, rather shyly, opens his jacket, revealing a solid gold 45 revolver. When Elliott asked if he could hold it, Elvis handed over the gun, advising him to be careful. It's loaded. I assumed it was quite heavy because Elliott handed it back rather quickly.

Elvis ended up inviting us to the basement of the hotel for a little after-party. Another memorable moment. Here we were, away from the glitter of Vegas to the most unglamorous of location. The basement of the hotel. Aged pipes overhead, and below a long old wooden table containing a smattering of hors d'oeuvres, booze, and sixteen or so guys and girls awkwardly interacting.

Off in a corner, Presley, Elliott and I sat talking life for quite a long time. The loaded gun and why it was needed, never came up. It seemed to carry no room in any of our thoughts. My impression of Elvis was —if you knew this guy, how could you possibly not like him. He was so forthcoming, so sincere, so sweet, so kind-hearted, and so 'trapped' in this basement.

He made us feel so free, so light, so able to roam to our hearts content, that we just wanted to lift him up and whisk him off with us. We, of course, knew this was not realistic. Elvis couldn't walk free. Anywhere. Not without being mobbed. The price of fame shouldn't feel so sorrowful.

Even though Elliott and I hadn't known Presley before, we felt a little heartbroken when time came to leave him. That feeling, while sad, helped me to appreciate where I was at. You didn't have to be on top of the world to feel blessed. I carried no heartache. Until that moment I never realized how strong that was. Simple 'gets' make a world of difference. I was learning.

Elliott Gould

Elliott Gould, while basically shy, was always trying to discover who he was, and never shied away from meeting new people. In fact, he took it on more than anybody I've ever known. It was a constant for him. Here I was, the more outgoing of the two, but shied away from meeting new people. A contradiction for sure, but that's how it was. Most of us are somewhat hesitant when it comes to the unknown. We don't exactly embrace it with open arms. Who knows where it leads. Better to just play safe, and let it pass. Not Elliott. A restless searcher willing to go through the 'uncomfortableness' to find whatever he needs to find. He's certain about his uncertainty and it drives him forward. Thanks to him, I always reaped the benefit.

Elliott would call and say, let's visit Jimmy Durante, Groucho Marx, retired legendary UCLA basketball coach, John Wooden, Reverend Schuller of the Crystal Cathedral, etc. The list could go on and as varied, it didn't matter. Elliott loved to bring them soup and rice pudding, and it was always appreciated. Well, mostly. There were two times we ran into unexpected negatives.

Once Reverend Schuller asked Elliott if he would mind having a little chat with him at his congregation in the Crystal Cathedral. Elliott saw nothing wrong with the request and graciously accepted. Later, Elliott told me he drew some flack from the Jewish community for doing so. It had never occurred to either one of us that this was going to be such a sensitive issue. Since we were kids, we couldn't remember a time we ever spoke about religion. This was serious stuff, and we were both pretty naive as to people's feelings on this level. Elliott was just offering good will, with a side order of soup and rice pudding.

The second incident was a bit bizarre. The fact that it took place at a house Boris Karloff once owned, (now rented by Elliott), has little to do with the story, other than it might have made Karloff laugh. Just the thought of seeing 'Frankenstein's Monster' laugh it up, would have been a sight to see. Anyway, there we were at the 'Monster's' house, when Elliott sprang up, saying he had to go out for awhile. I didn't inquire why, and off he went. About an hour and a half later, he returns with lox, bagels, and Groucho Marx. Groucho was wearing a little French beret, and appearing a bit out of it. I don't remember him saying a word as Elliott led him to the couch, seated him, and started to unwrap the lox.

Like many, I was a big fan of the Marx Brothers so this was a treat, even if it didn't come with a hilarious Groucho quip. I think I might have tried to make some small talk with him, but Groucho's eyes remained longingly locked into the lox and bagel.

A few minutes later, there was an urgent knock on the door. Elliott opens it, and in rushes a totally hysterical woman in her late thirties, Groucho's caretaker. She furiously yells at Elliott for 'kidnapping' him from his home and bringing him here. Groucho was unruffled, trying to get a bite of his bagel, when she forcibly stops him. Then screams at Elliott, "Salt can kill him! Salt can kill him! How dare you do this", and so forth.

She proceeds to lift Groucho from the couch, who hasn't stopped reaching for his bagel, and hustles him toward the door, still berating Elliott for not knowing better. As she slammed out, Elliott and I just looked at each other. I could already read the morning headline: ELLIOTT GOULD KILLS GROUCHO MARX AT BORIS KARLOFF'S HOUSE USING SALT.

Jack Nicholson

Speaking of headlines...I still wasn't in them. But I was off to Eugene, Oregon to do a smallish role in a picture called *Drive He Said.* Jack Nicholson's directorial debut. Jack felt that since I was into gambling and knew so much about sports, I would make a great play-by-play basketball announcer, who also did interviews with players and coaches.

He was wrong. Those things were an art in itself and I sucked at both. If I had been cast as the 'color man', it might have been right up my alley, but doing play-by-play was a nightmare. It required rapid fire players names, doing all kinds of basketball maneuvers, done in real time as they run up and down the court. No script. Just wing it, while keeping it speedy and exciting.

In other words, be a pro. Trying to go as fast as I could, while making up players names off the top of my head, was akin to animal cruelty. Somebody should have brought an elephant gun and shot me on the spot. Interviewing the winning coach after the game (played by Bruce Dern) didn't go much better. I should have started the interview by telling the coach that I have a serious migraine and would have to cut the interview short, as in 'Nice game, Coach, but I've got to get the fuck out of here for everyone's sake.' Other than those tiny blips, I really enjoyed my time on the movie. I know you probably want to hear more about me, but I think a few words about Jack Nicholson is in order.

The friggin' guy is contagious. It's hard to walk into a movie theater and not fall prey to his infectious sense of style and charm. It shouldn't come as a surprise that Jack became a big movie star. As I stated earlier, predicting who would become a movie star wasn't my specialty, but Jack reaching that level, was not only a giant surprise to me, but also to many of our friends.

His early work in Roger Corman B films and others showed such a lack of promise that I remember saying to one of our pals, it was so obvious Jack would never have a future as an actor, we shouldn't even kid him. His work was so wooden and downright boring, we just thought of him as hopeless. What made this mystifying was the Jack we knew was just the opposite. Full of colorful flavor, flow and likability. Who was that stilted impostor up there on the screen??

Well destiny has a curious way of making amends just before all is lost. Actor Rip Torn pulled out of the movie *Easy Rider* last minute, and the powers behind the film, Dennis Hopper and Peter Fonda, turned to Jack. Little did they know they had sheer dynamite on their hands. With a little help from his friends and 'un-inhibiting weed', Jack did more than get by. Swinging for the fences, he unleashed the Jack we all knew, and the rest was history.

Jack relished his fame. Besides being bright, shrewd and irresistible, he was a showman. Jack wasn't satisfied to just captivate his audiences on screen, he was after them wherever or whenever the opportunity presented itself. I'll give you one incident to illustrate what I'm talking about.

One Sunday Oregon morning, we decide on doing a rafting trip that happens every year; almost everybody in Eugene participates. Buoyed by some tokes of 'Mary Jane', plus a few bottles of brandy, off we go in water beyond cold with our rented raft. Me, Jack, actor Bill Duffy, writer Bob Towne and Julie Payne, Towne's girlfriend and daughter of movie star, John Payne.

The trip was considered a walk in the park, but as we shoved off, the current was faster than we thought, and the river deceptively more shallow. So much so that after about a hundred yards, the bottom of our raft is ripped open from jagged rocks below—along with Jack's wetsuit. This was actually an alarming development, because we had to straddle the raft for two more hours before the pick up point. I think we were all feeling a little too mellow to realize the predicament we were in. Julie immediately recognized the haplessness of her crew and took on the role of

198

boat commander, barking out orders on how to shift and turn and whatever. Girl power showing itself even then. The biggest danger we faced came in the form of a large floating log with dagger-like spikes.

As we were rushing toward it, Julie yells out "Go under! Go under!!"

We all managed to do that, but when I surfaced both the lenses on my prescription glasses were gone. How the hell that ever happened without damage to my eyes will remain a forever mystery. Some walk in the park. That event was canceled permanently after rumors that four people didn't survive.

Nevertheless, during the entire trip, as Jack's ass became bluer and bluer due to the frigid water, he never failed to 'moon' other rafters as we went past. Be it parents, grandparents, kids—it didn't matter. Jack was going to leave his 'audience' a memory they wouldn't forget, and he loved every devilish moment of it. There's just something in his DNA that says, I got you where I want, and I ain't letting go anytime soon. That strong sense of self, plays an important part when something comes along that could rock your very foundation.

In 1974, Time Magazine research department turned up some stunning news on Jack's upbringing. The woman who raised him as his mom turned out to be his grandmother. And the woman he thought was his older sister was actually his mom. That's a nice bit of news to be dumped into one's lap. Jack's attitude was basically—Thanks for the share. Called it a pretty dramatic event, but nothing traumatizing. Said he was pretty well psychologically formed. Ironically, the movie *Chinatown* was soon to be released, which had it's own level of identity conflict.

What made this whole story kind of amazing was— back in the days of the Hollywood softball league, Jack and I both played on a team named Darin's Demons, sponsored by our #1 fan, Bobby Darin. Barbecues at his house after every game, with his wife Sandra Dee and Bobby cooking up a storm. Nothing was too good for the boys. Okay, ready? Not until Darin was 32, did he learn that the woman who raised him as his mom was actually his grandmother, and that his older sister was his real mom. Are you kidding me??

Unfortunately for Bobby, he didn't handle it as well as Jack. It drove Bobby into seclusion up at the Big Sur, where he lived in a trailer for nearly a year. Bobby died five years later at 37 years old. A year before 37 year old Nicholson found out the truth about his family. Neither man knew each other's history. Talk about the odds on that one.

Since I'm on the topic of Nicholson, there's one more story I feel the need to tell. WARNING: It's loaded with drama and heartbreak. During one of our Hollywood softball games, a ground ball is hit to our second baseman. As I run over from shortstop to take the force out, the throw is dribbled in the dirt toward me, which forces me to bend low to make the out. Wham! I receive the runner's knee in my face, full force. This was serious. The blood was running amuck. I was hemorrhaging. The ambulance was called, the whole deal. I knew it was bad, and the tone of voice from my teammates confirmed my own medical evaluation.

"Hang in there, Joey. Hang in there. The ambulance is coming real quick, hang in there, kid."

There I was, possibility going down for the count, and my biggest concern was the rescue of my glove. It had taken me four intensive months of hard work to break it in just the way I wanted. I knew it would be forgotten in the ensuing chaos. So I plead with teammate Nicholson, who's hovering over me with words of support, to retrieve my glove and keep it safe.

He assured me he would, but I begged—"Please Jack, don't forget. Please." It was like a dying man's last request. You can't fail him.

I spent two days in the hospital, my nose packed beyond belief, only to find out Nicholson forgot my glove. I hope to this day there's still a little part of him that feels bad. If he doesn't even remember it, he'd better lie to me about that.

A Turning Point

There are certain days in life that are so defining you can replay them in your mind for years to come. For me, it was the day my agent set up a meeting to see a well-known director named Peter Bogdanovich, for a role in his upcoming movie, *What's Up Doc?*. I didn't have very much in the way of expectation. Go up, see how it goes.

As I entered Bogdanovich's office, he's reading a newspaper. Lowering it, he wordlessly points to a seat in front of his desk. It's a large impressive office, so it takes me a few seconds to arrive and seat myself. It's at that moment I notice that I'm looking up. His desk seems to be on a higher platform. Feels a little awkward, but it is what it is. Looking down on me, he says with sheer boredom, "So tell me about yourself."

I knew right then, this interview was going to be an uphill situation, but hey, what else was new. I was about to find out. As if on cue, soon as I started to speak, he raises his newspaper and starts to read again. Now I knew that show biz could be a little difficult to take at times, but this was a level I had never dealt with before. As I'm talking, I'm thinking this guy has to be the biggest...(fill in the dots) on the face of the earth. This was beyond a person being out to lunch. Wasn't even a question of basic respect. I just didn't exist. This was unacceptable on all levels.

It took my dignity five seconds too long to quit telling my life story to the back page of a newspaper. Peace had gone south. The upcoming blow would be going through his Los Angeles Times to his unconscious face, and would add the final touch to a non-existing show biz career. I stood up, raised back my arm to deliver the goods, when something stopped me midway…I was straining. Everything in me wanted to follow through, but I didn't…or couldn't. Lowering my fist, I abruptly turned toward the door and slammed my way out. Good chance he never noticed.

Reaching the street, my whole being was suddenly elevated. The sorry-ass guy who had left his apartment hours earlier was no longer there, and good riddance. When I arrived home, gone was the wooziness of rejection that had seeped in and sapped my energy. I had busted through an invisible veil of fear I never knew was there in the first place. Whatever confidence I'd lost in trying to secure a future was back in full force. I was reminded that after turning so many losing poker cards into winners, I never had to play victim to my circumstances. I had the power to alter any hand I was dealt. Yet somehow, I had allowed myself to go into the Bogdanovich meeting with the mentality of a loser. In terms of a prize fight, that encounter was over before it began. Subconsciously, I had thrown in the towel.

No doubt Bogdanovich had hit me with a cheap shot. One that could have knocked me out, but instead, woke me up! What could have been the end of a career, now felt like a beginning. There was still plenty in the tank to take me wherever I needed to go. When the phone rang it could have been anybody but I knew who it was. Strange, how we always seemed connected, even though we seldom connected.

"Hey pops, what's the good word?"

He shot back, "What's with the chipper...did you get a fucking job or something?"

That led to me telling him about my very big important meeting with Peter Bogdanovich. From my uplifting tone, Dad was anxiously jacked and said, "I hope you told him you did over 400 TV shows, have a gold..." That was my cutoff point.

"Hey, Dad, Dad, take it a little slow...Is it me, or do you add a hundred more shows each time you call."

He plowed right past that, "Stop the bullshit. Was it good or bad news?"

I told him it was a little bad, but a whole lot good. Said that the 'little bad' was I didn't get the job. But the 'lot good' was that I didn't punch out Bogdanovich. Dad told me to stop fucking around being funny, because only a moron would find it funny to LOSE OUT ON AN IMPORTANT JOB! I was about to explain how this day was in no way a loss, if one looked at it from a different angle, when he abruptly changed the conversation.

Seemed like he had just come from a doctor where he learned that his constant heartburn was 'not' due to all the greasy food he consumed. It was because of me, including the indigestion and rhythmic belching. I alone had upset his whole bodily system—besides ruining all his dreams. Even threw in that I had broken my mother's heart, which was massively untrue.

Regardless, my father was on such a hot roll, I never once thought of interrupting. God forbid he ever left out any unsaid communication that might clog up whatever was left of his arteries. It was truly a masterful performance, real meat on the bone that deserved some sort of recognition, but the punch line to the story was classically better. Later, via my mom, I learned the doctor my father had seen was a PROCTOLOGIST!

Now, either my mother was funnier than I thought, or this was just too good. All the crap my father hit me with, came from his proctologist?!

Anyway, when Dad finished talking through his ass, I calmly said, "Don't worry about a thing, Pa. My minds made up. Come Monday I'll be a whirlwind.

Well blow up Monday had finally arrived. It had a successful run, but its time had come. Dad went bonkers. "IT IS MONDAY! TODAY IS MONDAY!! IT'S MONDAY!!! MONDAY!!! MONDAY!!!! DO FUCKING SOMETHING!!!!!"

It took a moment for my hearing to return, before saying, "I didn't realize today was Monday, but if what you say is true, soon as we hang up, I'm going to immediately sit down and write a movie."

When I hung up, Dad's blowup just made me laugh. If anybody had walked in on me at that moment, I'd have a lot of explaining to do. After the laughter subsided, I sat for a long moment in quizzical silence. Why not?? If Jack Nicholson could sit down and a write a movie, why couldn't I? I certainly had a better bathrobe than the 'crappy thing' Jack once wore.

California Split

It's amazing how life works. It does its thing and when the smoke clears, you often find yourself in a whole new ball game. My father thought my gambling was sure to be my demise. Yet because of it, I went on to write *California Split*. I figured at the time, it was a subject I knew something about, so why not take a shot. What did I have to lose? Even if I was able to get through the writing process, the chance of it ever being made into a movie was a long shot. But since I've always been a 'dog' bettor, that didn't phase me in the least. In fact, it motivated me even more. I was always leery of supposed 'sure things', but put me in the underdog role and I relished it. Felt at home. Just having the odds stacked against me, was all I needed to spur me on.

California Split was a movie in the making from the day I was conceived. It just took thirty-seven years of experience to bring it to the screen. No intricate story line. No preaching or teaching. No deep hidden meanings. Just a movie about two guys, following their bouncing ball to wherever the action led them. Simple as that.

My gambling buddy and agent Guy McElwaine, told me it was one of the five greatest scripts he'd ever read and said if he couldn't sell it, there was no reason he should be in the agency business. To make me feel even better, he offered to bet me three hundred bucks he would get it done. I accepted the bet. It was a no lose proposition. Either way I was a winner. If I LOST the bet, it meant that *California Split* was being made, so the puny $300 would pale in comparison of what I would earn off selling the movie. AND, if I WON the bet (God forbid), I could shoot myself and later be found with three hundred rotten dollars in my pocket.

Guy also mentioned he had a client anxious to direct the movie. And since studios were starting to show interest in that client, maybe he could combine both elements to further the deal. As he said, fabulous new writer, and fabulous new director was a good selling point once he got a studio to buy into making the movie. While he was brainstorming, I had come to a conclusion that threw him.

Since he was so sold on the script, I decided to go for broke. I would be the 'producer' on the movie or no deal. As convinced as Guy was about getting the picture made, he was equally convinced he couldn't pull off the producer role for me. He said I had no background that he could base his argument on. This is where my gambling nature paid off. I told him to use any words he wanted in describing me. Call me crazy if need be, but if I don't produce, I'll just throw the script in the fireplace and be done with it. I don't know who's fireplace I was referring to but it sounded pretty good. To convince him further, I said if he couldn't do it, I don't want any last minute phone calls. Just flatly turn it down.

As uncompromising as it sounds, along with few funds in my pocket and fewer prospects, it wasn't a bluff. I'd been around the business long enough to know unless you had some power, you only had yourself to blame if things didn't work out the way you wanted. I wanted *California Split* to be *California Split.* Guy must have gotten the message because he pulled it off.

Daniel Melnick, the man in charge of motion pictures for world renowned MGM, said he loved the script. Thought it would make a terrific movie, and said YES to everything. Joseph Walsh could produce the movie, and a kid from the Monday night football crowd called Steven Spielberg could direct it. Naturally, the studio asked for a few minor changes, which was the norm on any movie, but the concept would remain as is. That's all I wanted to hear! From their suggestions, I could tell they had spent a good deal of quality time on the script, which was impressive. They really loved the non-movie reality of the characters, and just wanted to further enhance them in certain areas.

All of it was in keeping with what I had written, and it was a true pleasure working for and with these talented professionals. When the rewrites were completed, they were more than excited to get the project going. All they asked of me, was to consider shooting some of the Vegas stuff in Circus Circus, because they owned a piece of the hotel and could get a real good deal on it. That didn't bother me at all. In fact, I kinda liked it. My creative side just knew there would be something comedic about putting my 'two guys' in that setting. The execs were delighted with my reaction.

So there I was one morning, half-way out the door, when the phone rang. For a moment, I thought of not answering it. I was already late to meet up with an MGM exec at LAX airport, in order to check out Circus Circus first hand. But after the second ring, 'something' told me to answer it. Felt important...so I did. And it was. But not in a good way. It was Guy, telling me he was glad he reached me before I flew off to Vegas. When I inquired what was wrong, he told me he was in a serious rush and would let me know all about it a little later. Then abruptly hung up. I had a sinking feeling, and with my acute antenna, that was not a good sign.

What I ran into was worse than I thought. James Aubrey (also known as the Smiling Cobra) struck with full fangs. Being the President of MGM, he overrode his movie executives and informed them that all deals would be canceled, unless I agreed to make the movie his way. Said he could see the picture as clear as day.

These were the changes he wanted:
  —Singular Hero gambles,
      but ONLY against bad mob guys.
  —Singular Hero BEATS bad mob guys.
  —Bad mob guys get PISSED and
      CHASE Hero to Las Vegas.
  —A HAIL of GUNFIRE ensues at Circus Circus.
  —AERIALISTS freak,
      falling on BUXOM cocktail waitresses.
  —PANDEMONIUM breaks out.
      Maybe an ELEPHANT STAMPEDE
      if they have any elephants.

The 'serpent' saved the best for last. Dean Martin (Aubrey's close friend) would have to be cast in the leading role, playing the singular hero who gets shot, but is saved when the bullet is deflected away from his heart by a sliver dollar chip pendant he always wears for good luck. Also, I should rename his character to Chip Green and call the picture, *Lucky Chip*—<u>Oh, and I would no longer be the producer of the movie.</u>

Now I had heard about Hollywood horror stories before, but being in the midst of one was like having a mouth full of Novocaine. I couldn't feel my lips as I explained that he may have missed something in my script, because the characters I was writing about weren't heroes. They were just regular guys who needed to gamble to feel more alive—basically more

212

victim than hero. The cobra wasn't listening nor smiling. For a victim, he wouldn't give a quarter. For a Dino with a lucky chip, he would invest 2.4 million dollars. I refused. Here I was with my usual shortage of funds, and I just turned down 2.4 mil.

When a month went by without another nibble on my script, I also lost my director. Spielberg was always so energetic and highly supportive of my screenplay that it was disappointing when he eventually had to pull out. I couldn't blame him because 'Split' had gone cold, and Fox Studios had just offered Steven the chance to direct a big project called, *Lucky Lady,* starring Burt Reynolds.

Still it was quite a blow, and had my head reeling to a point where Dean Martin, a casting catastrophe for me, started to look infinitely better. He could even sing "That's Amore", and wear a shot glass around his neck if he so chose, that way having the bullet hitting his lucky chip WHILE shattering glass. Visual excitement. It might work. I was trying hard to see the new fit, but somehow the idea of crawling back to the studio and getting the Barnum & Bailey version of *Split* was finally too much for me to handle. Better to just drink a lot and lapse into a coma.

Home alone, I was envisioning cheap wine and $2 parlays deep in my future, when McElwaine showed up at my door, asking to be paid off for the three hundred dollar bet we made. This was sounding pretty exciting, but he wasn't telling me any more until he had the 300 bucks in hand. The bastard had me and knew it full well, god bless him. As I coughed up the dough, he told me that Columbia Pictures was excited to make my movie, and had absolutely no problem with me producing it. He said all the top executives at the studio were anxious to have a face to face with me, so they could personally welcome me to the Columbia Pictures family. If this wasn't a heart warmer, I don't know what was.

Seconds later, my heart wasn't feeling quite as tender when McElwaine added, they also want to talk to you about making a few changes. I immediately snatched back the 300 bucks. If this picture was going down the tubes once again, my three hundred wasn't going with it, that's for sure. Guy quickly assured my furrowed brow they were only talking minor stuff. They loved the script. All I could think was, so did MGM and then they sprang the Cobra. McElwaine assured me no cobra, smiling or otherwise. The change had something to do with just the opening scene. Not a big deal. When he said that, I instinctively knew what it was. Even when I first wrote the script, I kinda thought I would run into some trouble in that area. Shouldn't be a problem, but still held onto the three hundred just in case.

At the meeting, nobody was talking about changes. Everybody was so busy telling stories on each other, that it was definitely making me feel part of the family. After literally forty-five minutes of cavorting with my dearest of friends, they sprung the change they wanted. It was just as I suspected, and I was more than ready for it.

In the opening scene our two lead characters are in a card club, playing California low-ball poker. When we think poker, it's the highest hand that wins. In California low-ball, it's the reverse. The lowest hand is the winner. Ace, deuce, three, four, five being the best low ball draw hand you can hold. It's not a game played in most households when it comes to poker.

So one of the execs says to me, since low-ball is sort of exotic, wouldn't it be better if you changed the low-ball thing to regular poker, because then everybody could understand it. You know, like four kings beats four queens. I certainly could do that, I said, if you're looking to lose money. The exec was stopped cold. What did he just say?? I then launched into my theory of 'reverse commercialism'.

Ever since audiences have been going to the movies, all they're invested in is whether their screen heroes win or lose. Everything else is mostly beside the point. But in the case of *California Split*, if you dumb down the picture, you will turn off the gambling world, which is something you do not want, because 'that world' is much wider then they could ever imagine.

The ideal thing you want from that audience is for them to walk out of the theater, buzzing with the belief that they've seen a movie made just for them. That word would spread like wildfire (which it did) and we will be on our way to a successful movie. When I finished my reverse commercialism spiel, they all said, almost in unison, not to change a thing. Not a thing. I never knew if they agreed with all I said, but just the thought of losing any money was more than they could bear.

As strange things so often occur in Hollywood, Universal Pictures, who had Steven Spielberg under contract, decided last minute not to allow Steven to direct *Lucky Lady* freeing him up to direct *California Split.* Only it was a day too late. Movie maverick Robert Altman had just signed on to direct.

Robert Altman

Being a first time producer, working side by side with heralded director Robert Altman, was certainly an experience.

The first thing out of his mouth when I met him was, "You know, I'm supposed to be your mortal enemy."

Since I knew nothing of his reputation, I found it an interesting statement. "Why's that?"

"Because writers think I take their script and destroy it."

"Well, do you," I asked simply.

That seemed to throw him. He started fumbling some responses. Things like - "A script can't be restricted… Who's to say what may or may not be true…If we lose discovery, what's left?…What are words on paper but a mere sketchy blueprint," etc.

It all sounded heady enough if we leave clarity on the back burner, but that's not what bothered me. I didn't mind him free-wheeling his higher wisdom until the words—MERE AND SKETCHY entered the conversation. After spending well over a year to get the script where I wanted it to be, and have it dismissed in such a cavalier manner, was flirting around in sneaky-but-lethal-left-hook territory. He went on to say that Ring Lardner Jr, creator of *Mash,* hated what he had done to his script, but was more then happy to accept his Academy Award.

Although I didn't realize it at the time, a lot of his opening volley was based on a few things that were working against me. First of all, when my agent sent Altman the script, he stated his belief that it was his top five greatest reads. Second, when Columbia green-lit the picture, they stressed to Altman how much they liked the script, and would like it to remain as is. Even though Altman agreed with all concerned, in retrospect, I realized they were fighting words for him. No one tells him how to make a movie. It just goes against his grain. And lastly, which he didn't hesitate to say, and I quote, "Who the hell are you to be producing this film on an equal basis as me? I don't get it."

He certainly had a point there. But didn't tell him how I played real hard ball on that issue.

I simply said, "I have a good agent. What can I tell you."

To say Altman didn't like me producing the movie on equal terms, was an understatement. He couldn't seem to get over how I'd pulled off such a good producing situation, and never failed to complain about it whenever it crossed his mind, which was often. I also suspected he didn't like that I couldn't be intimidated by him, which never did stop him from trying. I could understand it, but trusted he would soon get past his ego, and it would all work out fine. This was to be a big lesson for me in how power operated.

In the beginning, we were tossing out names as to who might be good casting for our two male leads, so it felt collaborative. I thought my buddy, Elliott, would be great in the role of Bill Denny, but Altman immediately nixed that. He'd worked too much with Elliott Gould. "Too much Elliott Gould" he repeated. He was so adamant about having someone else, it felt like a closed issue. Shortly thereafter, it was decided we would go with George Segal in that role.

Now we had to find someone to play the Charlie Waters role. A charismatic character that I considered far and away the best part of the two. I heard from a friend of mine who'd read my script, that I should see a small movie that had just opened, called *Mean Streets*. There was an actor in it that could be perfect to play that role. So that afternoon I went to see the movie, and my friend was right. The guy was terrific! Just knocked me out! So I got in touch with his agent and had him bring in Robert De Niro to meet Altman.

It turned into an awkward twenty minute meet. I felt it was because Altman didn't know the actor, but when De Niro left, Altman passed on him right away. I suggested he see *Mean Streets,* because this guy was pretty special in it. But Altman wasn't interested. Somehow I sensed that I'd talked up De Niro a little too much for Altman's liking, and his dismissal of De Niro had more to do with me, than it had to do with De Niro. I knew right then that this collaboration process would still have to go through some growing pains. Altman was top dog. That was being made clear to me. Okay, I got it. But what happened next wasn't okay.

Steve McQueen

Steve McQueen was the biggest star in the world at that time. He'd read the script and wanted to have a meet. This was to take place in Freddy Fields office at Creative Management Associates (CMA). Freddy just so happened to be the biggest agent in the world, and represented McQueen. As I'm getting ready to go, Altman informs me that he'd rather take the meeting with McQueen without me. This was a real slap in the face. 'Equal producer' was being left behind to think about how power worked. I didn't like it.

One hour later, I got a call from Altman, who tells me to get over to Freddy Field's office right away. Didn't tell me what for, or why. Just get there. As I walked into Freddy's office, the atmosphere felt a little grim. No one bothered to say hello, or even introduce me.

McQueen just walked up to me and said, "In this movie you wrote for me, my character isn't hep enough. This Segal guy you've already cast, has the best part and all the hep lines. My part has to be written much hepper if I'm expected to do it."

Well, this threw me on all sorts of levels. First of all, it was news to me that I had written the movie for

McQueen, because he never once entered my mind. I suspect that misinformation came from his agent in an attempt to butter up McQueen's ego. Secondly, the word 'hep' had left the scene thirty years ago. And lastly, I considered the character of Charlie Waters to be THE role in the movie. So hip, in fact, that I didn't quite know how to respond to McQueen. If I said hip instead of hep, would it sound like I was putting him down? Something too hip to a hep kind of guy? I was in a pickle. I knew I couldn't afford to get into some 'vessel with the pestle' routine, but the more we talked, the closer I got to 'the pellet with the poison's in the flagon with the dragon'.

Here I was, in the middle of the biggest meeting of my life, and as I started to riff on the mercurial character of Charlie Waters, I could feel McQueen's confusion. We just couldn't seem to connect on any level. I told myself that things weren't going as bad as it seemed. At least he wasn't talking about clowns and bearded ladies. He was busy berating Segal for having a hepper role in a movie supposedly written for him.

As I was struggling to get through to McQueen, describing the character's uniquely 'hep' qualities as one-of-a-kind—the word SNOWFLAKE popped out of my mouth. Today that 'word' seems to have caught fire in the public with various usages. But back then, a snowflake was a snowflake, plain and simple. But apparently too way out for McQueen, because his eyes glazed over, and I saw he was going under. It was criminal. I had slipped him the pellet with the poison, not the brew that was true.

McQueen quickly responded—"I don't understand a freakin' thing you're talking about. I gotta go and buy Ali hats." He headed for the door, but turned back with a final comment. "I don't do paragraphs. Just write me hep one-liners."

With that, the biggest star in the world, a man of few words, walked out. I assume to buy his wife, Ali MacGraw, hats.

Soon as the door closed, Freddy Fields, known as a tough guy, charged to within inches of my face, snarling like some gutter bully, "YOU CAN'T TALK TO STEVE MCQUEEN LIKE THAT! YOU CAN'T TALK TO STEVE MCQUEEN LIKE THAT!!"

Well, that's all it took. Being bullied in anyway was like waving the proverbial red flag in front of the bull. The confrontation was on. Either the bull is taken out, or the matador is carried out. I had little to no control of my reaction. Outcome was never a consideration.

"LIKE WHAT," I said, "LIKE WHAT!!"

My snarl carried so much intensity, it blew Mr. Fields back a foot, instantly lowering his tone to somewhat acceptable, "He's a simple guy, He's a simple guy."

"Do you mean he's a SIMPLETON! Do you mean he's a SIMPLETON," I shot back.

In our fiery upset, both of us had fallen into a pattern of repeating the same line twice. Stupid talk, but that's the best we had to offer. It would have made for a great scene in some movie, but unfortunately this was real life and the meeting was a complete and utter disaster.

Yet somehow it didn't end there. That would come the following evening when McQueen came to the office we were using in Westwood. Altman was to screen him his last movie, *The Long Goodbye,* starring my buddy Elliott, playing Raymond Chandler's famous P.I. Phillip Marlow. When McQueen arrived, he seemed proud to say, this would be a first for him, because he'd never seen an Altman movie. This I'm sure had Altman skipping with joy. From there, it went straight down hill.

As the movie started, McQueen, like a wind-up doll, never stopped talking: Why is the character doing that...what's he doing now...what did he mean by that... did you shoot that in Malibu...I used to live there...that water out there can get cold at night...Is the Gould character playing a cop?

I could see Altman's face getting redder with every question he answered, until he finally cracked and said with a stone grimace, "You're watching the movie, Steve. You figure the goddamn thing out."

When the movie mercifully ended and McQueen had left, Altman was livid with rage. He lambasted McQueen for all he was worth. Nitwit, moron, idiot, etc. etc. Altman, who didn't say ONE word during the thirty minute McQueen/Fields assault, now couldn't contain himself. He ended by saying McQueen couldn't be in *California Split* if he got down on his hands and knees and begged for the part. I never said ONE word during Altman's tirade.

A day later, my agent called to tell me Freddy Fields and Columbia Pictures were furious, and blaming me for losing them the biggest star in the world. They said that I deliberately poisoned 'Altman's well', and they hated me for it. I couldn't believe what I was hearing, but in another way it didn't surprise me. Growing up in the streets of New York taught me that power thrives on the weakest link in the chain. That's just the way it is. Better to come away with a lump or two, but just stand your ground and you'll be fine.

I truly believe that the earlier Freddy Fields encounter helped *California Split* become the movie I wanted to see. Although Altman never spoke of the blow-up between Freddy and myself, he had to realize I was not going to be a pushover. Yet Altman still had another power play up his sleeve.

Holding My Own

As I walked into Altman's office one morning, he immediately blurted out that he'd cast the role of Charlie Waters. Everything in his tone said that it's final, whether you like it or not. He proceeded to tell me he'd called Elliott Gould in Germany, where he was finishing a movie, and gave him the role. This was a complete reversal on his part. He had nixed Elliott when I first brought him up. Too much Elliott for him. Now, without ever telling me, he goes ahead and hires him to play the wrong role, as I saw it.

As Elliott later told me, the first thing he'd asked Altman after being offered the role, was if I was alright with this. Altman said I knew nothing about it yet, but that's the way it was going to be. Elliott explained to me why he knew he could do the part, and why I never got it.

"Growing up, you were always the Charlie Waters' character to my Bill Denny. But as far as the rest of the world was concerned, I WAS Charlie Waters."

He was absolutely right in every way. I was dead wrong. Elliott Gould was born to play that character.

As fabulous as that casting turned out to be, Altman's message to me was clear. It read—whatever producer position I was in, meant little to him. He was the boss, so stay the hell out of his way. If I didn't get that on our first meeting, it was being hammered home once again. Altman was not the subtle type. Let me take a moment to demystify the role of movie producer. It's not brain surgery. You don't have to go to school for a number of years to qualify. It was clear to me from the opening bell that working in the Robert Altman universe was going to be a challenge. The count was 0 and 2 before I even stepped to the plate. I got the picture.

But I knew from experience that I was good under pressure, had basic intelligence, and knew how to read people due to loads of hours playing winning poker. Without those skills I was ripe to be eaten alive. That didn't happen. Anytime Altman suggested something so far out of left field, I would question it. If he couldn't come up with a good reason for the change, I would calmly explain my motivation for the scene, and how sometimes it had taken weeks, even months to get it.

I caught on early that he was trying hard to take the importance out of the written word, and that was fine as long as he didn't screw things up while doing so. These conversations never made him happy. He would storm out the door on so many occasions it was funny. Funny, because they took place in his office and I knew he always had to come back.

There was one time in particular that I really got to him. After a particularly bizarre idea, I actually said to him, "Oh c'mon, Bob, if you do that, they'll laugh you out of the theater." That was the biggest door slammer of them all.

When Bob gave interviews, he would always like saying the phrase, "I just giggle and give in." That wasn't particularly true. Bob was more like a big kid, who if he couldn't get his way, got pissed, then got over it reasonably well. Being arbitrary, based on very little, was just part of his makeup. He was a guy who lived to make art, especially movies. When he wasn't filming something, he wasn't a happy camper. Yet whenever he did interviews, he went out of his way to 'put down' Hollywood executives. Referred to them as the SUITS, as if it was a dirty word.

This made no sense to me, so I asked him why he had to go out of his way to knock the people that paid his bills. He basically just said, they know nothing except how to interfere, and besides it made him feel better. To which I responded, "Are you going to feel any better if you're never hired again?" He countered, saying he wasn't worried. There was always going to be somebody who would come along, needing some class in their lives.

Teamwork

Regardless of personalities, Altman and I were growing to like and respect each other, and started to work as a team. A few weeks before the movie was about to film, I asked Altman if I could write random background scenes that wouldn't interfere with the main scene, but instead add a level of vitality and reality that 'movie extras' could never supply. I knew a lot of good actors who would love to work for Altman in any capacity, so working background would never be a problem for them.

I also knew through the grapevine that he hated working with extras, so thought his reaction would be positive. It was. If I was willing to put in the additional labor, he thought it a fabulous idea. Every inch of the screen being 'alive' with humanity really turned him on. So much so, that one day he came with an idea that he said, would work perfectly with mine. He wanted to mic-up all the background actors so as to hear snippets of their conversation. Sounded great to me.

This whole new dimension being added to the movie was pretty exciting stuff. Too exciting for our poor sound guy. After a few stressful days of trying to raise, lower, and mix sound, he fainted dead away. Fortunately for all of us, he recovered and we went on to make some movie history. *California Split* was the first non-Cinerama film to use eight-track stereo sound. Rather than hire any extras for the racetrack and card parlor sequences, where a great number of people were needed, we used Synanon members, an organization for ex-addicts. After what these people had been through in life, we knew the film would become more alive with just their presence. We were right, lucky, and thankful to have them.

As the days went on, Bob and I continued to roll. It became less about WHOSE movie was going to be made, and more about WHAT would make for the best movie. We still bucked heads over certain things, but it was now feeling less personal.

Although, speaking of personal, there was an incident that took place on the movie set, that was quite a hoot. In the picture, I play the role of a bookmaker (wonder who cast me), who harasses Segal over some gambling money. One of my two scenes in the movie is a phone conversation where I wasn't on camera, but which I loved doing. I was in Altman's office, hooked up to a phone in our second floor office where the scene was actually being filmed. While I'm tearing into Segal over the money he owes me, in walks Freddy Fields. The same snarling Freddy Fields of 'YOU CANT TALK TO STEVE MCQUEEN LIKE THAT' fame!

As I glance toward him, he looks somewhat surprised to find me there instead of Altman, but I continue the scene, never once dropping out of character. Freddy looks like he doesn't quite know what to do, but after a beat, sits down on the sofa. Because my scene is long, and plays so real and tough talking, I see Freddy start to squirm. I know he doesn't realize he's walked into a movie scene, and here's that guy again who he hasn't seen since our explosive encounter in his office, laying heavily into someone over some money issue. Even though I was totally involved in the scene, the humor of the situation wasn't lost on me. I just knew Freddy Fields was thinking, 'Who the fuck is this guy?!' Freddy was supposed to be the biggest and toughest guy in Hollywood. Who in the world is this confident, hard-nosed little pisher?!

Whatever was going through Freddy's mind, he became so uncomfortable that halfway through the scene, he rose, gave me a meek little apologetic wave and whispered in a tiny voice, "Tell Altman..." He stops, thinks, then headshakes to forget it. With that, he left in some sort of tip-toe fashion so as not to disturb me any further. I really doubt that Freddy Fields ever found out it was just a movie scene being played out. At least I hope not.

Go Produce!

When we finished shooting in Los Angeles, we were off to Reno to complete the picture, where still another power play by Altman took place. This one, however, had a more amusing slant. One day, lights were being set up in the casino for an upcoming scene, so Altman and I sat down to play a few hands of blackjack. Before long, the first Assistant Director approaches us with much concern regarding four African American women from the NAACP, demanding to talk to the director, or producer of the movie. Their issue being why aren't there any black people in the cast. Altman peeks out from behind the dealer and sees some seriously hefty ladies, intent on getting to the bottom of this.

Without hesitation, he turns to me, "You're a so-called producer. Well, here's your chance. GO PRODUCE!"

"Okay," I say, "but they're asking for the director or the producer, and you're both."
"It's your goddamn life story. Tell 'em whatever the hell you want."

With that he abruptly gets the hell out of Dodge without waiting for the dealer to pay off his winning Ace/Queen Blackjack! I thought of keeping his payoff just for lamming out like that, but it just wasn't my style.

As it turned out, the meeting went great with the ladies. I took them to a wonderful breakfast, told them my life story and how there was no discrimination intended. There were just no people of color involved in my story. Everything I told them was true and we got along famously. They even asked for my autograph and couldn't wait to see the movie. While escorting them out, I suddenly remembered something that would surely please them further. I was about to hit them with the good news, when I stopped myself. Maybe it wouldn't be that wise to tell this story.

There's a scene in the movie that actually happened to my brother in real life, which I thought worked perfectly for the Charlie Waters character. While leaving the racetrack, I have Elliott and company getting held up at gun point by a guy demanding all their money, and Elliott only willing to give him half—Take it or leave it. My only problem in telling this story to my new fun friends was…the hold up man was BLACK. True story or not, I just didn't feel this was a good way to end such a lovely breakfast.

Later that day, after relating my success with the ladies to Altman, and giving him his blackjack winnings, he was in a really good mood, so I mentioned that Thomas Austin Preston Jr was in town. Mr. Preston, famously known as Amarillo Slim, was a legendary poker/gambler figure that everybody in that world knew, or had a story to tell about. Since Altman was very happy with me that day, he didn't hesitate when I suggested getting Amarillo Slim to play himself in our big poker sequence in Reno. Bob just said, sounds good to me.

When I met Amarillo for breakfast, Slim never let me down on all the things I'd heard about him. Wearing his trademark Stetson cowboy hat and his Ostrich Skin Boots, he dripped with colorful flavor in just about everything he said. He was born in Johnson, Arkansas, moved when he was young to Turkey, Texas, then after his parents divorced, his mom went back to Johnson and his dad moved to Amarillo, Texas. That was great by him because it was a helluva lot better to be known as Amarillo Slim, rather then Arkansas Austin or Turkey Tom.

We also shared a laugh over W.C. Fields antics in movies where it concerned poker. W.C.'s attitude was never give a sucker an even break. Slim commented that he would never look for a sucker. Instead, he would look for champions and make suckers out of them. He'd recently won the World Series of Poker to back up his point.

After many more stories, I was prompted to offer up a bet I knew he couldn't refuse. Slim was always known to accept a bet where he knew the odds were in his favor, so I reached into my pocket, plunked two hundred bucks on the table, and said I would pick ONE NUMBER correctly in the next Keno game. If he wanted the bet, he'd only have to put up three hundred. Since there are eighty numbers in play and only twenty numbers are called each game, the odds were in Slim's favor.

"You got it, son," he said.

Then pulled out (what I had heard about, and was hoping to see,) a humongous wad of $100 bills, held together by just a rubber band. The bulk of his bankroll was so large that a normal person's hand would never be able to fit around it. Peeling off three one hundred dollar bills, Slim asked me what number I wanted. Without hesitation I said the first number that came to mind—Number Nine. A minute or so later, the Keno game was on, and the first number that flashed up on the board was Number Nine!

As I casually picked up the five hundred bucks, Slim told me that was down right spooky. He then pulled out his incredible bankroll to give it another try. He'd put up six hundred to my four hundred, then asked me to state my number.

"Zero," I replied immediately.

"There's no zero in Keno," he said.

"I know."

He smiled. I smiled back.

"So I take it, we don't have a wager?"

I shook my head. "Afraid not, Slim. Just couldn't forgive myself if I made a bad bet twice."

He gave me a gentle but curious smile and said, "I'm not sure if I can read you yet young man, but I kind of like that. Just tell me what days I'll be shooting your movie."

Having signed up Slim gave me a good and comforting idea. George Segal, whom I had not previously known, had virtually no gambling experience prior to the film. Because of this, I mentioned how invaluable it would be as an actor, for George to play No-limit Texas Hold 'Em with legends Amarillo Slim, Sailor Roberts and various seasoned players, using his 'own money'. That way he could really experience the pain of the loss. George, of course, won all the money that night. So much for brilliant thinking.

One Special Lady

When the day came to start filming the big Reno poker game, the feeling had been elevated due to one special lady who had just arrived to play the barmaid in the scene. When we use terms like boundless energy, ray of sunshine, bundle of joy, we're talking of Barbara Ruick. Such an infectious spirit to be around, you couldn't help smiling and feeling things were going to work out just fine. Thus was the energy that filled everyone's space.

Even though it was close to 20 years, I could still picture her singing WHEN I MARRY MR. SNOW in the movie *Carousel*. Not long after that, she had graced composer John William's life by marrying him and blessing him with three beautiful children. The Altmans had been good friends of Barbara and John for years, so when Bob asked if she would like to come out of retirement and play the role in '*Split*,' she was ecstatic.

After being away from the business for so long, she was literally overjoyed at the thought of performing again. The word was that Williams wasn't keen on her doing the movie, but relented when he realized how happy it made her. After meeting Barbara, I could understand John's feelings. Losing her for even such a short time couldn't have been easy. Losing her for all time was more than John could bear. The day she completed her role, feeling so elated, turned tragic by nightfall. She suffered a cerebral hemorrhage and died in her hotel room.

Experiencing John's loss the following day was painfully sad. As Altman and I stood there talking to him, he was nowhere to be found. Trance-like disbelief had taken him to such a far away place, I wasn't sure if he knew we were there, or what was being said. That incident stayed vivid throughout the years, and just recently I watched an interview in which Mr. Williams was asked, if there was ever a personal moment in his life that affected his work. When he was forty, he responded, he'd lost someone very very close to him unexpectedly, and before that point in his life, he hadn't known what he was doing. After that loss, he felt clear about what he was trying to do in his writing and approach to music, and could do it. He went on to say it was a huge emotional turning point in his life, and one that still resonated in him some forty years later.

Without mentioning Barbara Ruick by name, he said it was the greatest gift anyone had ever given him. Calling it the most pivotal moment in his thinking and the living of his life, and most certainly when it came to his approach regarding the blank page. He seemed to know immediately where to go with the emotion he carried…On the final credit roll of California Split, it starts with—*For Barbara*. After *Split*, John Williams went on to compose the music for *Jaws, Star Wars, Schindler's List*, and many other great scores. I knew the depth of where that music was coming from— I was there.

A Life Ending Gamble

Upon completion of our movie, Altman and I watched the finished product together and were more than impressed. We celebrated with a drink, then off I went for a few days with my second wife, actress Barbara London, who was so wonderful in *California Split* as the lady who throws oranges at George Segal at the racetrack. We were going away to see if anything from our relationship could be salvaged. It never really worked from the start and had gotten worse over the years. No one to blame. It was just the way things go at times.

What made it all worthwhile though, was the birth of our two wonderful daughters, Kelly and Josie. What a pair of loves they were, and still are as adult women. If the marriage was a mistake, they certainly weren't. I have always adored being their father.

A few days after a trip that spelled the end of my marriage, I returned to the office to encounter a most morose-looking Robert Altman, holding an early morning drink in hand. He had just watched *California Split* and said that it was the worst movie he'd ever seen. I can't tell you how thrilling that was to hear. Where did the picture go that we were so impressed with a few days earlier??

The very next day when I returned to the office, he was beaming from ear to ear. He'd just finished watching the picture again and thought it was the best movie he ever made, and possibly the best movie ever! If there was any way I could have stolen the print so he couldn't watch it again, I would have done it.

When *California Split* opened in New York, I was there with the publicity guys at 5 AM in the morning, anxiously waiting for the New York times Vincent Canby review. Canby, at the time, was considered the dean of movie critics and vital to the success of your picture. Turned out he loved it, saying it was truly a one of a kind. Columbia guys were ecstatic and despite the AM time, called the head of Columbia Pictures, who was awaiting the news. David Begelman had recently taken over the studio, and *Split* was the first picture he green lighted. So this was a very important moment for him.

As the publicity guy is delivering the best news Begelman can hear, he also mentions that I'm standing right there next to him. I could tell right away that something negative was said, because the publicity guy's tone and conversation suddenly turned awkward. When the phone call was over, I pressed him on what was said. Since we had grown tight on the trip, he told me, although reluctantly, that Begelman said if I was standing next to an open window, shove me out.

Despite the great news, Begelman still couldn't let go of the false notion that I had lost him Steve McQueen.

Hopefully he took comfort with the worldwide critical acclaim and profitability of the film, even if he wasn't as delighted as me when I won a Writers Guild nomination. Canby came through even further at the end of the year, naming it as one of his top ten films of the year. This was a huge honor. With all the movies made in the world, he picked *California Split*...My God! Wasn't it time for David Begelman to bury the hatchet on something that wasn't true. It never happened.

This bothered me because I really liked the man. I found him to be an ultra classy guy when he headed ICM. We had spoken often, and even went to the racetrack on one occasion, along with movie director Martin Ritt. Marty owned a few horses, and on this day his trainer talked up a filly that had worked good. Might be worth a wager, but nothing to go nuts over.

This was key speak for a guy like me. This type of tout usually would see the horse run 4th or 6th. I bet sixty bucks on him, which I felt was fifty too much. Marty went for a hundred, and Begelman passed altogether. I remember feeling that's a wise man. As I headed off to lose my sixty and Marty's hundred, I'm met half way by Begelman. He tells me he's decided to bet the horse, then slips me TWO THOUSAND DOLLARS!

"Put it on the horse to win," he says, "and don't mention this to Marty.

I found this quite surprising on two levels. This horse, according to his trainer, clearly wasn't worth such a sizable bet, and Begelman was never known to us as a gambler. I made an appeal to his senses, but to no avail. I made the bet for him. The horse ran 5th and that was the end of it. Another losing day at the racetrack. What else was new.

What happened to Begelman a few years later was ironic, sad, and on one level, a new first. Turned out that David was a closeted big-time gambling addict, who was so seriously in debt to his bookies that he shamed himself by stealing actor Cliff Robertson's per diem money. How in the world could a head of a major motion picture studio take such a wild and desperate action?? It didn't make sense even to someone like me, who knew well the pitfalls of gambling. There had to be another way out than the one he took. It was crazy. Not only did it cost him his job and reputation, a few years later he went totally broke and took his own life.

People who claimed they knew David well, often commented there were absolutely no clues to be found that he was capable of such an act. Called it a complete mystery. For me though, there were clues. The first was the secret two thousand dollar losing bet at the races. The second and probably the biggest, was when he landed the top job at Columbia Pictures. Right away, you're under the gun to do well. It's hugely important that the first picture you do is a success. Something close to surefire is the way to go. You certainly don't pick a high risk gambling movie to secure your future. Yet that's exactly what Begelman did when he green lit *California Split.* Was he compelled? Did he really know something? I don't know the answer to that, but his instincts proved correct.

Throughout the years, when Begelman comes to mind, I always think of him fondly. Without him, who knows if my script would have ever made it to the big screen. He believed in something that has grown in stature to where it's now viewed as a film classic, and widely considered the best gambling movie ever made. Thanks David, for what you did for me. Rest in peace.

A year after *Split's* release, I ran into Spielberg, who brought up the movie. He told me he would have made a whole lot more money with the picture (which was probably true due to Steven's uncanny commercial instinct), but graciously said that he couldn't have made a better movie. That showed some real style on Steven's part, and meant a great deal to me.

No, No, This Can't Possibly Be Happening!

While *California Split* had brought me all kinds of accolades, it was also the setting for a most REMARKABLE LIFE EVENT!

My on-camera scene with George Segal is one I have never forgotten. When Altman said, 'Cut. Print', I felt mortally disappointed. I hadn't achieved what I wanted. This was a complete surprise because I'd never taken acting to heart on this level before. Up to that point, I was just an East Side kid who had gone further than anyone had expected, with little assistance from me. When my father stopped me from becoming a professional prizefighter, I was just going along for the ride, wherever that took me. I wasn't future oriented in any way, shape, or form. So feeling this down was something I hadn't experienced before.

Segal knew how I felt and tried to tell me how wonderful the scene was. But I wasn't buying any of it. I just wanted to go home, a most defeated 'little kid', which I'm sure is what prompted George to ask 'how old I was'. A simple question, which required a simple answer. Thirty-seven.

As I opened my mouth to tell him just that, some kind of altered consciousness took over, and years started tumbling away in rapid succession. Twenty, forty, hundreds?! I was literally unable to speak. In my minds eye, I was being transported back in time to wherever, and until I arrived, there was nothing to say. It was like a roll of film being rewound at increasing speed. I couldn't quite make out the faces and places, but clearly saw ashen ruins as centuries flew by.

As much as this was mind-blowing stuff, I also knew it was an impending disaster. Part of my brain that wasn't heading back to god knows when, knew that if I didn't give George an answer real soon, everything I had going for me at the moment was in real jeopardy. Here I was, back to a point in the 'business' where I mattered again, and the reality of reincarnation was being introduced to me. No, no, this can't possibly be happening!

Joey, tell him you're thirty-seven before this gets serious. It doesn't matter if you've been here before; this big news flash doesn't come with rent money. What are you going to do—tell him you're 647 going on whenever?! That should go over great coming from a first time writer-producer talking to a movie star. I could already hear Columbia Pictures telling my agent, "Your client must be replaced. He's got 'One Flew Over The Cuckoos Nest' problems."

As my trip through time started to noticeably slow down, George repeated with alarm, "Joey, how old are you?"

With that, before I could open my mouth, hundreds of more years went crashing past, and I was left speechless once again. I knew I freaked out George. I could sense his fear. A moment later he was gone.

The how or why I was given a glimpse into a distant past was truly astounding, but clearly dangerous. I wasn't an imbecile. I knew beyond a shadow of a doubt I'd been around the block a crazy amount of times, but who would buy it? I lived in the real world, and in the real world, you don't suddenly announce you know all about reincarnation. My career was in the cross-hairs of being shot down, and I knew I needed to return to the production office as quickly as possible—OR I wouldn't be producing *California Split* another day longer.

Lucky for me, George didn't bring up the incident. As I sat there waiting for the dailies to be shown, I was lost in thought about what had happened to me. I knew how extraordinary it was, while also knowing I could never tell anyone on the movie about it for fear of damaging repercussions. As the lights dimmed, I was soon in for another huge surprise. Segal was right. The scene that started all the unique drama was terrific, and I was doing the best work of my career. Go figure.

248

Even though George and I remained friends, I didn't bring up the incident to him until a few years ago at the Telluride film festival, where *California Split* was being honored. I felt it was about time he knew the real story and would be truly fascinated. But to my surprise, he still felt uncomfortable talking about it, so I just let it be. In fact, throughout the years, I've only told a handful of people about it, mostly family, because I never felt the need to convince anyone. Although it did send me to book stores to find out about reincarnation. I couldn't believe how many books had been written on the subject. Seemed like what happened to me wasn't a rare occurrence. There's a belief out there that everybody has gone through reincarnations whether they know it, believe it, or otherwise.

I wasn't about to shout it from the roof tops, but it shifted something in me. There was more going on than I previously knew—and I liked that. Who knows what people had to get through to reach where they were today? At the very least, it made me more tolerant. Getting caught in judgments about others lost steam as I became more forgiving.

I also began to view time differently. It wasn't running out on me like some doomsday scenario, which took the pressure off the finish line. I didn't have to 'rush' to be anything other than myself. Time became more of a friend. Life wasn't just a big crapshoot after all. It had levels of awareness, that if I cared to stay tuned, would serve me well. The urge to keep taking unnecessary risks remained (I'll get to that), but emotions over the results changed for the better. I looked at them differently. Became more grateful for a win, and less negative to a loss. It began shaping me in a way that felt newer and more alive.

It's certainly more comforting going through life, realizing you failed many times before, and will again, and what's the big deal? It's not the end of the world. It felt freeing to know I have a lot more mistakes in me, so just relax. Do my best and let it go at that. It was good my confidence was in a solid place because life was about to hand me a few other surprises.

The Old One-Two Punch

After *California Split* I was sought out to write projects for every major studio. The one that came through loud and clear was adapting the novel, *The Raging Bull* to the screen. When Martin Scorsese offered me the job, it was exciting on two levels. One, I loved Scorsese's work. And two, it was a story about the life of Jake LaMotta, a prizefighter. What could be better than that! The man who had bought the rights to the book was none other than Dino De Laurentiis. The same man that had produced *Anzio* back when I was a lowly actor in no demand whatsoever.

What I didn't know at the time was that Mr. De Laurentiis held writers in such low esteem, he paid them dirt cheap prices back in Italy. I quickly learned the truth of that when he offered me LESS money than I made for *California Split*. This was unheard of after a successful debut. Everyone was paid more, not less. On Split I made $65,000. De Laurentiis offered $55,000 to write *Raging Bull.* My agency told him that even though I looked forward to working with Scorsese, he had to offer me a deal that made sense. Not only did De Laurentiis not come back with another offer, he lied to Scorsese, saying I asked for an exorbitant amount, while also adding he felt I didn't want to write it.

None of this was discovered until much later. Needless to say, it was depressing when I found out about the horrible lie. I really believed that Scorsese and I would have made a great team. Not only for *Raging Bull*, but for years to come. We never crossed paths again. The movie was eventually written by Paul Schrader, who did an absolutely wonderful job. And Scorsese directed it into a great film. I'm sure my services weren't missed, but still, lies can hurt.

Right after that, I was offered the job to adapt Peter Gent's football book, *North Dallas Forty*, for a fair and decent price. They also told me that Bob Altman would direct it.

"Great," I said, "I'll do it."

The following day, Altman called me about it. Asked if I would do him a favor.

"Sure, name it."

Much to my surprise, he wanted me to back out on writing the movie. I was so stunned by this request, all I could get out of my mouth was—if that's the way you want it, no need to talk further. Call it pride, bewilderment, or any other emotion, I wouldn't, or couldn't, bring myself to even ask for his reason. I don't know what went down later, but Robert Altman didn't get to direct North Dallas Forty.

Despite my newfound success, the world was proving that I'd better be ready for anything. Although I must say, what happened next was such a surprise, it took my breath away.

Rumble in the Jungle

The Rumble in the Jungle—Muhammad Ali vs. Big Bad George Foreman. How good can it get? So much excitement was coursing through me that I shadow-boxed in front of my bedroom mirror to get ready for it. My right hand was explosive and true to the mark. My sneaky-but-lethal-left hook looked sensational. My footwork was nothing short of breathtaking. So dazzling, the title was mine for the taking, until I suddenly landed flat on my ass. My fabulous, new, slipperier-than-shit Italian shoes had been my downfall. What a break for Ali-Foreman. They could now concentrate on each other because they didn't have to worry about me anymore.

Lifting myself off the 'canvas', a profound certainty came over me. Something really big was going down tonight and I was going to be part of it. My excitement level grew until it was off the charts. Strange because I WASN'T BETTING ONE DIME ON THE FIGHT! The compulsive gambler in me was nowhere to be found. I was back to the innocent kid who didn't need a wager to have his heart crushed. A baseball announcer supplied that in 1951. I can still hear Russ Hodges' voice screaming at me: "The Giants win the pennant, the Giants…" No…no…let's not go there. Forgive Ralph Branca. Let Bobby Thomson's 'shot heard round the world' mercifully fade from memory.

This was here and now, and for the moment I was one PURE fight fan! I was so turned on by this event, I wouldn't let my brother miss it. It wasn't a hard sell. He was delighted to go, especially since I offered to spring for dinner, fight tickets, late night drinks, the works. I was flush, so money was no problem. At least, that's what I thought at the time.

When we arrived at the Wilshire Theater in L.A. for the closed circuit live broadcast from Africa, the atmosphere was electrifying. My brother wanted to go right in and get a seat, but for me it was too soon. There was such a wild, excited energy filling that lobby that I didn't want to leave it. Mistake. Big mistake. While I was busy soaking it all up, I spotted a bookmaker who owed me money. I know that's a switch on the norm, because it's almost always the other way around.

The guy was a small time bookie whom I'd beaten for several weeks, but nothing big. Highest bet he ever took was $200. He basically owed me nothing, something like 250 bucks, but still in all, I didn't like getting stiffed by a BM. It just wasn't the way it should be. Yet, feeling so sky high and not wanting anything to interfere with that incredible space, I'm ready to dismiss the guy altogether, when some 'distant' part of me suddenly speaks up. "Listen Ed, I gotta go see a man about a few dollars," and off I went.

As I reached this guy, I say in a very easy manner, hey, how ya doing? And he says, none of your business, so fuck off. Whoa—talk about a reply. I wanted to blast him right there, but kept my composure.

"Are you kidding," I said, "don't you owe me some money?"

"Get a lawyer," he shot back. With that he turned away, completely dismissing me. It felt like the back of his head was crying out to be pummeled, but hitting someone from behind just wasn't me. Besides, this was Ali and Foreman's night, not Walsh and Bookmaker. Still, I was seething over the arrogance and nastiness of this creep-shit and couldn't let it go.

"I don't know where you're coming from, pal, but you're way out of line."

The creep-shit turned back. "Really…well if you don't like it, we can take this right outside."

This was not what I wanted to hear, nor was it acceptable.

"Why don't we do that," I said. Stupid, I know. Sometimes when you're faced with a level that's intolerable, stupid prevails.

When we got outside there was a mob of people milling around, so he suggests we take this around the corner where nobody could break it up. I was keenly aware this was going too far, but never hesitated. We went halfway around the corner in total silence, until we reached a ramp where trucks went down to a cargo bay.

"Let's go down here," he said.

This felt like the arena from hell, but there was no backing out for me at this point. With my adrenal system pumping like a madman, I went down the ramp. When we were completely out of sight, he turned and charged me like a freight train. I threw a punch, missed, flew in the air, and for the second time that evening, landed on the deck, thanks to my new slipperier-than-hell Italian shoes.

But this time was no laughing matter. In an instant, he was on top of me, his elbow stuck in my throat, pressing down for all he was worth. *There was no way I could breathe.* Worse yet, there was no way I could tell him I couldn't breathe. I'm not sure it would have mattered to him, but I would have liked the chance to explain my dire situation. I just couldn't believe it. Something was all wrong with this picture. This dude owed me money, for God sakes, not the other way around!! Talk of a bad beat.

It's pretty crazy what your mind goes through when you're facing your final breaths. It was really tripping. Besides the heightened whirl of anger, fear, and remorse about loved ones, there was also—I hate fucking Italian shoes—Boy is my brother going to be surprised—I hope they put this cocksucker in the electric chair and then hang him—This works for Columbia Pictures; they'll make more money on my demise. I could already see the headline: *Berserk Bookie Kills California Split Creator Over Chump Change.* All these thoughts appearing simultaneously, but each clear as day as the light was fading fast. There I was, knocking on obits door, when a drop of sweat fell from my assailants brow and hit me square on the forehead. It must have been made of Holy water because suddenly his elbow released my throat and he seemed to vanish in thin air.

I lay there perfectly still...strangely feeling panic for the first time. It seemed like an eternity before I was able to catch even a smidgen of air and realize that from being a 'dead loser', I had come all the way back to the win column. Speaking as a gambler, that's always a great feeling.

Eventually, I returned to the other fight with a torn sport jacket, painful hip, sore throat, and sheer luck at finding my brother in a darkened theater. As I slipped into my seat, he turned with whispered annoyance, "What the hell happened to you?! I thought you were going to miss the fight."

"Yeah, I know," I replied casually. "Got caught up in the prelims."

I thought my remark was pretty cool under the circumstances, but it flew right over his head as Ali and Foreman walked toward the center of the ring to receive the referee's Marquis of Queensbury rules. Basically, no low blows, no rabbit punches, no hitting a man while he's down, no sticking elbow in opponent's windpipe and choking the shit out of him, etc. The ref ended his spiel by telling them good luck, touch gloves, and come out fighting.

This felt so civil and majestic compared to my dirty little street fight. I'd been through these type of deals before, and they were ugly, dangerous, and degrading. As the bell sounded for Round One, Ali and Foreman headed toward each other. Their fight made sense. They were fighting for glory and millions, but where was my payoff? My Rumble in the Jungle was fought for nothing and nobody.

Reining in the Warrior

The following day, as the world was raving over Mohammed Ali's sensational knockout of big George Foreman, parts of my body were aching from my pathetic street encounter, while my mind was already in dismissal mode. It's over. Forget about it. Life was practically screaming at me and there I was trying to side step it. What's with that? Last night I was within seconds of being dead. Jesus Christ...Is it possible for you to give that a little extra thought?!

As I stared at myself in the mirror, movie star Paul Newman popped into my mind. I was remembering him playing the part of the real life story of professional fighter, Rocky Graziano. The title of the movie was— *Somebody Up There Likes Me*. It was like receiving a message, telling me that I was lucky to have clout in higher places, but quit pushing it. We have limits.

While lost in that stream of thought my phone rang. My agent was calling to tell me that I was offered the job of writing about a guy who couldn't seem to be killed. The timing of all this had my head spinning. I knew my alley fight was not only dumb and beneath my intelligence, but more importantly, a little beyond my control. Maybe there were some survival tips in this material that would come in handy.

After reading the novel LEGS, about gangster Jack 'Legs' Diamond, I could see that the best thing Legs had going for him was some odd belief that he might be invincible. Surviving so many stabbings and shootings puts peculiar ideas in the head. It served as an appropriate warning. Rein in the warrior part of my nature, or I may be joining Legs very soon. That stupid alley fight the night before left me angry, but hopefully wiser. I had two little kids, and almost left them without a father. I told myself, THIS COULD NEVER HAPPEN AGAIN, but wasn't convinced I would succeed. Knowing that inner forces can take over in the blink of an eye, I had to be super vigilant. My job was to write about Legs, not join him in some miserable end.

When I finished the screenplay and the movie was set to be made, starring Roy Scheider, with Walter Hill directing (both men at the top of their game), the studio got last-minute cold feet. Someone in the organization became convinced that after *The Godfather* films, the genre had run it's course. *Legs* was dead.

After spending so much time bringing characters to life, you become attached, so it's not easy having a lot of your 'personal friends' rubbed out just like that. The studio paid for the hit job, so end of story. I got it, but it still carried somewhat of a body blow.

Spielberg

Getting worked up over the loss of some murderous bootlegging gangster was kind of funny when I gave it some thought. Jack 'Legs' Diamond was a really bad guy, but boy did I miss not seeing him up on the silver screen, doing his best to make an audience feel for him.

While nursing a tear for the demise of Mr. Diamond, Steven Spielberg thankfully stepped in and left *Legs* in the dust. He hired me to write a screenplay, based on a true story about a Brink's security guard who robs his own truck. Basically about a young guy who is at heart a dreamer and finds love on the lam. Despite us not doing *California Split* together, Steven and I had never lost our connection because of how often he'd show for Monday night football.

Since I was considered the gambling guru for the Hollywood elite, Steven would always ask what side I was betting, and invariably I would give him a hundred dollars of my action. This happened four to five times and I never lost. Since he never stayed for the completion of a game, I would always pay him a few months down the line, which was always met with gleeful surprise. So much so, I wondered if I lost, would he ever remember to pay me?

Couldn't care less about the hundred bucks. It was just a thought, because he was so far removed from my type of gambling. Covering a spread on a football game was so meaningless to Steven, I'm sure it was forgotten the moment he left the Monday night fanatics. It was always clear to me that his heart, soul, and passion were funneled into one thing. Doing a movie and making it work.

Much as I had gotten over 'not' becoming the welterweight champ, I saw how passion carries it's own tail winds when it comes to knowing exactly what you want, and how to get there. Steven's direction was always power driven and straight ahead. Mine came with detours, but that fit well with my gambling personality. Uncertainty acted like a stimulant. It's like when I was a kid and it came to the 'grab bag' gift. I was excited about unwrapping the unknown item. The gift itself seldom amounted to much, but it didn't matter. I was expecting the unexpected, and that was the turn on.

There was one particular surprise that was totally unexpected and ridiculously rewarding. When Spielberg completed *Close Encounters Of The Third Kind, he* asked if I would do him a favor. Come in and make up dramatic background dialogue that he could insert into the movie. It was suggested a nice case of wine would be sent as a gift. That would have been great by me, but it would have gone against my actor's union rules; so instead I asked to be paid actor's scale of $179 for the day. I knew a case of nice wine was going to be a much richer deal, but sometimes, albeit grudgingly, it pays off to do the right thing. The movie turned out to be such a big hit, I've lost count of how many tens of thousands in residuals I've gotten, and still get to the present day.

The same situation arose when Steven produced *Poltergeist*. He asked me to come in, on camera this time, and enact our real life Monday night football ritual for the opening scene in the movie. Since the others were mostly top executives and high price agents, Steven wanted me to drive the scene, ad-libbing anything I wanted. For this generous gesture, he would send all a nice case of wine. Having learned well, I said send the others the wine, but just pay me the measly scale. Thousands of dollars in residuals followed, thank you very much.

The only thing I felt bad about was my first ad-lib, "Who the hell is this guy?" This was in reference to our football game suddenly disappearing off the TV screen, and *The Mr. Rogers* show replacing it. I knew exactly who Mr. Rogers was, because I religiously watched his show every day with my precious little girls. But for the character I was creating in the moment, the line felt right and Steven loved it! Since I knew the type of scary movie Steven was making, my next ad-lib of

"I bet my life on this game," sent Steven over the moon. Easy stuff for me to enact, because there was many a time I felt that pressured about a wager I couldn't afford to lose.

Curious thing about that movie. The morning of the shoot, Steven introduced me to Tobe Hooper of *Texas Chainsaw Massacre* fame, who was supposed to be directing the picture, and that's the last I saw of Tobe. For the next two days, Steven directed every moment of it. And from what I later heard, continued in that capacity throughout the entire movie. Although when the movie came out, Tobe Hooper was credited for direction.

****

Before tackling the story of the Brinks kid, I was to fly to Texas to meet a certain drug Kingpin, who had befriended the kid while he was on the run. All had been arranged by Kingpin's lawyer, who had pitched Spielberg the story. When I arrived in Austin, a very serious looking guy picked me up at the airport, and drove me into the hills somewhere to a pretty fantastical house where I was greeted by the Kingpin. Already the whole thing felt like 'I wasn't in Kansas anymore,' but that was only the beginning.

When I asked him to describe the Brink's kid, he simply said, "Cops and Robbers."

I gathered he meant not a real crook. More of a play actor. Certainly not a serious man, but the kid had a good heart. Kingpin liked him. Because his lawyer had vouched for me, the drug lord began to elaborate on many more things than he should have, legally speaking. I was being trusted like a family member.

I surmised he had a lot of young children, because there was a gigantic playpen in the living room the likes of which I'd never seen. I figured the wife and many kids were not around because of our meeting. I was mistaken. At one point, he asked me to stay for dinner, then after, join him in the playpen for some dessert with the young ladies he was having over. It was said so easily, so no big deal, that I immediately felt like a prude.

My refusal had to be first rate. It would have to match or surpass his casualness so as not to offend. In asking for a rain check, I may have gone a touch overboard because playpens and me were sounding like a match made in heaven. I made it feel like, if I wasn't so exhausted from my flight and all, I'd be diving in head first. He didn't give it a second thought, inviting me to talk some more the following day on his $20,000 speed boat the cops-and-robber's kid gave him as a present.

It was only when I was about to leave that his whole demeanor took on a darker tone. He stood inches from my face, said he liked me, BUT - if I ever turned out to be 'undercover'...he would cry his eyes out. At that moment, tears were rolling down his cheeks. Let's just stop for a moment and think. What would you do in a spot like that? What would you say??

"Who me? A copper?? Nah!"

"Hey, I hear you. I wouldn't like that either."

"Oh, c'mon, Kingpin, why would I be one of those."

"Not to worry. Trust me. I'm who I say I am in spades."

I can't quite remember exactly what I said, but think I settled for the old standard, "What?"

The following day he took me for a ride on the Speed Craft, paid courtesy of Brinks. Just me, Kingpin, and two other guys who never spoke a word. It wasn't exactly a relaxing day, because I was trying my best to dispel any thought of me being an undercover agent. After all, I was in the middle of a lake; and yes, sleeping with the fishies was a long shot, but still these guys didn't feel like strangers to that sort of behavior.

Let's just say I was looking forward to dry land, when suddenly a voice from seemingly out of nowhere, cries out—"Joey...Joey Walsh!"

Who in the world is calling out my name in the middle of a lake in Austin, Texas?? I was completely flabbergasted. Kingpin and his associates went rigid. I realized from their point of view, they smelled a trap. The air was suddenly filled with tension as a speed boat pulled up alongside us.

I recognized a guy from my agency ICM (International Creative Management). When he asked what I was doing there, I told him I was working on a project for Spielberg. It was just normal chit chat meant to ease the tension I was feeling from Kingpin.

All was good...until he said, "Hey man, do you have any grass you can spare?"

At the time, a request like that wouldn't have been a big deal, but under the circumstances it hit like a bomb. The trap was in. I WAS UNDERCOVER!!

I could feel the itch on some trigger fingers as I quickly told the ICM guy, "No drugs. No drugs of any kind. This is purely a work trip."

He registered disappointment, and off he went. The day was saved, but not right away. The suspicion on our craft was still palpable, and I acknowledged it. I told the Kingpin that I came on the boat ride feeling the need to dispel any idea that I was undercover, and someone just happens to be on the lake calling out my name, asking for drugs?? How bad was that? I remember being quite humorous on how I related the situation. No one laughed, except me. But Kingpin believed my explanation and that was good enough. I got out of Austin alive, with plenty of good material for the movie.

Soon as I was back in California, I was off to Lompoc prison to get a personal feel of the Brink's kid before attempting to write about him. He was a wide-eyed idealistic young man, who was thrilled that someone was doing a movie about him. I'd never been in a Federal Prison facility before, so it was quite fascinating. We met in an extremely large visiting room, where many inmates were being visited by their wives or girlfriends. Everywhere I looked, they were squeezing their lady's breasts as they talked. It was an extraordinary sight. I also spotted H.R. Haldeman of Watergate shame, who was loved by everybody in prison, according to the Brinks kid. He was doing ton's of paperwork for their appeals. Haldeman was no dummy. He knew how to protect himself in prison.

After my penitentiary visit, it was time to put pen to paper. Since I didn't type, I agreed to write the movie from Spielberg's home, where his secretary could type it and give it to him to read as we went along. I wasn't sure how this would work out in the beginning, but since Spielberg was so gleefully complementary toward my writing, he kept me inspired for months on end. He never said a negative word about any scene I wrote. The only way I knew it was off the mark for him, was after giving it glowing remarks, he would add, "… but I just feel you can do a little better with this scene."

Whatever natural talent I had as a writer, he always extracted more from me, without ever mentioning what was missing or needed. In short, Spielberg's talent antenna was so fine tuned, it served as a gift to me.

When our movie was ready to be made, he wanted to squeeze in one other picture called *1941*, a kind of satirical disaster film. The thing that made him hesitate was it's level of humor. He didn't think it was that funny and asked me to read it, and give an opinion. This was a loaded request. How could I give an honest opinion about a screenplay that would take the pole position over mine? This was a true test of character, but I decided on being a stand up guy.

If the script warranted it, I would give it the thumbs up. In fact, I started to become enchanted by my sense of integrity and was already rehearsing my speech before I even made the read. 'Steven, *1941* may not be *Gone With The Wind,* but it sure as hell deserves to be made. Mine can wait.' I could already feel the pride swelling in Spielberg's chest toward me. All I want from now on is to make a million movies with the honorable Joey Walsh.

Steven's first instinct was right, however. It wasn't very funny. My shot at nobility had vanished, but this was certainly a great development for me. My project quickly jumped into the lead. Could we be ready to shoot in twenty days, Spielberg asked, and I said no question. It's good to go today. A week later, he called and said he's going with *1941* and would I do him a big favor. He would give me $20,000 to come along with him on *1941*, and whenever I saw a chance to make it funnier, to buzz his ear. It certainly wasn't an ideal situation, but I didn't want to let him down.

I didn't have to worry, because he never called or spoke of that deal again. He shot *1941*. It didn't turn out too well. And my project with him never found the light of day.

The Driver

In Hollywood, broad shoulders are a necessary requirement. All romantics (writers), save your sad stories for the unemployment office. A line from the Godfather movie summed it all up perfectly—'It's not personal, it's business.' Just suck it up and move on.

That soon arrived when Walter Hill, director of *Hard Times, The Warriors, Streets Of Fire*, and the Eddie Murphy big hit, *48 Hours*, called to ask if I would come see him. During the meet, he told me about his next film, *The Driver,* which would star Ryan O'Neal, and asked if I would play the lead villain in it. I wouldn't have to read or test for the part. Quite an offer.

This was a gutsy decision on his part, and I told him so. What a switch. An actor trying to create doubt in a director's mind as to whether he should be hired. It didn't faze Hill in the least. He wanted me for the part. Just say yes and that would be it. Wow. Lead villain. Still, I was somewhat hesitant and said, "I believe I can offer you *California Split* type performance." He said perfect. That's all he wanted.

Maybe it was better I'd been away from acting for some time, because my work on *The Driver* felt fresh and completely at ease. On one particular day, I had a five minute scene where I barge into one of my 'bad guys' apartment while he's in bed with his girlfriend. I had so much dialogue to remember it could easily intimidate. But not that day. Moments before Director Hill called action, I had such a serene sense of peace, it felt like something new was about to transpire. I can't quite remember at this point what I did, but I knew the work was special. Somehow, I had reached a powerful level of truth never experienced before. It didn't feel like acting. Even though I was playing a bad guy, it just felt like glorious joy and I wished it would never end.

When Hill informed me there had been a technical problem and the scene would have to be shot again, he was sick. Walter loved what he'd just witnessed and felt terrible that I would have to do it again. Not so for me. Acting had never felt so sublime. I couldn't wait to do it again. Wound up doing it twice more, each time coming in with a totally different interpretation of the scene. Hill and the producer raved, and I went home feeling like I was floating on rarified air. It's amazing what can happen when you're totally free of restriction and fear. It was like—where has this been all my life??

To top it all off, the following day I got a call from my close friend, Alan Ladd Jr. (Laddie), truly one of the most loyal and best movie guys Hollywood ever produced. I thought it was going to be a discussion about football, which we did on a regular basis.

Instead he surprised me by saying, "What's going on here? They just saw dailies of a scene, and told me you're going to be a movie star."

Since Laddie was head of motion pictures at Fox at the time and had green-lit *The Driver*, this was a real head spinner. This was coming from a man who had given us so many great films: *Braveheart, Alien, Blade Runner, Thelma and Louise, Chariots of Fire, The Omen, Norma Rae, Julia, Young Frankenstein, The Turning Point, A Fish Called Wanda, 9 to 5,* the list is endless. Laddie was also the one who said 'yes' to *Star Wars* when everyone was passing on it. Later, when it became a gigantic hit, all other top movie executives fell into a horrible case of amnesia. None remembered it reaching their desks.

Anyway, as Laddie waxed on about the dailies, I tried to downplay all my feelings, but it was a real turn-on. Who was this person everyone was so excited about? Show me. I couldn't wait.

The night the movie was set for a private screening, I was trying hard not to get caught up in all the possibilities this movie would do for me. I told myself to relax, because with all these in-house, out-of-this-world reviews, I certainly knew I couldn't be bad. I was just hoping the hype wasn't overrated. As the screening ended, I sat there stone silent. Not wanting anyone to see the expression on my face or the feeling in my

274

heart, I left before the house lights came on. The night-to-remember scene had been cut from the movie! Expectation had nailed my ass in a big way. It's like being dealt four aces, only to feel the impact of losing to a straight flush. I can't recall where I went that night, but it must have been a dim place to fit my mood.

The story told to me later was that the movie was too long. And no matter how much they trimmed, it still came up five minutes more than the powers that be wanted it. So the producer's wife spoke up, 'Get rid of Joey's scene.' Supposedly the room was stunned. She continued, 'I know you're all so enamored with the scene that its become untouchable. As great as it is, it doesn't move the plot along, so if you cut it, there's your five minutes.'

The woman that every guy had a secret crush on, including me, won the day. Oh Maggie…Why did you have to break my hopeful heart like that?

At fifteen years old, I never gave a second thought to Lee Strasberg and the Actors Studio when they used the word potential. Now, having the very best of me as an actor lay on the cutting room floor, never to be seen by anybody including myself, was a tough one to get past. Normally, howling at the moon over setbacks was not my style. But this felt like someone had snatched a glorious future from me, and run off with it. What a crime. Call the police. I was definitely having a hard time.

I never had ambition to be an actor, let alone a movie star, so what was this about? Where was my perspective on this one? I hadn't been given a terminal diagnosis of brain cancer. I just didn't get something I really wanted. Boo-hoo. Somebody hold a benefit for my feelings. That was the hapless state I was in— and felt every right to remain as lowdown as I wanted. The world wasn't interested in my drama, so let me pick up the level of care needed for the situation. Did I need a week, a month, a lifetime?

Selfish thinking to be sure, but I knew if I didn't allow for the grieve, it would stick to me until I did. Better to look it square in the eye, recognize that it got the better of me, thank it for the insight, and show it the hell out the door. At least I could see it as a nice break for Marlon Brando. If I hadn't wound up on the cutting room floor, he might have easily turned into an afterthought.

Over the course of time, I was still being well paid to write projects for the studios, but as Bob Dylan once sang—*The Times They Are A Changin'*. Many of the fearless types, who were the decision makers years prior, had been replaced. Corporate had moved in. Getting to a 'yes' became ultra serious business. If the new folk said yes and the movie failed, the clock immediately began ticking on who would become the next studio head. Fear ran rampant. 'No' became a lot safer than yes.

Other top writers that were in demand caught on real quick to what was trending and began making a fortune doing rewrites on other people's work. I wasn't as savvy as they were and took a pass, even though I was being offered a ton of dough to do them. In truth, rewrites would have been much easier, took less time, and I was better suited to it. Steven Spielberg touting that I wrote the best dialogue in Hollywood, certainly didn't hurt. But no, for me, it had to be an original. Hubris to be sure, but I bought into it. Despite being highly paid to create anything I wanted, the process was always long, and when the movie wasn't made, I just didn't feel like writing anymore and that was it. Left my agency, and never signed with anyone again.

Choice

Having reached the age of eighty-two with a clear mind and healthy body is a pure gift. Whatever I did or didn't do, whatever I accomplished or didn't accomplish, hardly matters anymore. Through the years I've come to realize that everything I encountered helped to shape me into who I am today. Both negative and positive forces played a valuable and equal role in teaching me how to go further. Some guy in a crummy bowling alley came within inches of slashing me into disfigurement or possibly killing me. Should I look at him as a bad guy, or an angel in disguise? He convinced me I had no future in New York. Pushed me through a door I needed to get through. Not that I understood it at the time. I was too busy believing I was in control of it all, to pay it much attention. I was long on confidence, which was a good thing, but short on wisdom, which was the main thing.

Whatever 'awareness' that surfaced always hinted there was more coming if I didn't insist on having things my way. My intuitive side had already shown it knew something my intellect didn't. Whether in gambling or in life, it had proven itself more reliable than any other ability I had. It brought with it the sense —don't worry, do your thing, make your mistakes, we've got your back.

The more I was willing to listen, the more I received. Staying in the moment and learning not to RESIST what life offered was a key.

Over the years, what it served up to me was a trust that everything that happens, holds secrets of value if unattached from good or bad. It was the type of belief that allowed for choice. And I 'chose' to accept the Universe as a near and dear friend, who only had my interest at heart. Good, bad, or indifferent, it was in my corner all the way. There was no iron-clad proof that was the case, except life seemed to work better when I didn't automatically throw a flag on how things went down. It wasn't easy when gripes, sorrow, anger, and all the rest of ego's cohorts were looking to break down the door if it didn't get it's way. When you're armed with only deep breaths and varying degrees of faith, the creatures of doubt are a tough group to fend off when all they're focused on is someone or something to blame.

Toss in the fact that they can't be terminated and never take a day off, you can see why it's important to stay light on your feet in face of unfriendly fire.

It's good to report, having found myself up close and personal with their fight plan, I've become much more effective on how to deal with it.

Don't want to say I've gotten the upper hand, but liking my chances more and more every day. Hanging tough, having fun, and just grateful to be along for the ride.

Final Thoughts

Dancing with the ego on any issue took a back seat when it came to my children. They were always front and center for me. It's amazing to think of the power kids possess. Throwing yourself in front of a train to save them becomes a no-brainer. They cover so much ground in your being that it's hard to think of life without them. It's like, please God, let me stay here long enough until they don't need me anymore. I've come to believe kids enter the world to raise you, just as much as the other way around, maybe even more so. They work like magic. You don't have to understand the 'how or whys'. They bring a smile to the face, wonder to the mind, and so much love to the heart, that it's easy to become a gushing fool.

If I wasn't blessed enough to have them, in 1977 I hit the 'death-do-us-part jackpot.' Barbara Gail Lightstone was more than I could or would ever want. Beautiful...Caring...Intelligent...Talented...I could easily go on, but I'm afraid I'm already in trouble when she reads this. Compliments have never been easy for her to handle.

In addition to the beautiful, spectacular Kelly and Josie, was my soulmate's three-year-old son, the brilliant and handsome Ryan. If that wasn't enough gift to bestow on one man, a few years later, Barbara Gail graced my world with the beautiful, glorious, Kathryn the Great. Two extra treasured kids to love and behold. It's easy to say your family and loved ones are the most important things in your life. But feeling it on a day to day basis, gives you whatever you need for what comes next.

With a rooting section like mine, it's difficult, if not impossible, to not give it your best shot. Thanks guys for a support system that keeps me flying ever higher. Wherever I go from here, I go with a humble heart.

Besides my family, one of the sweetest memories that never seems to fade is the morning *California Split* was to begin filming. I pulled up at the location to see a street lined with honey wagons, filled with cables, lights, camera equipment, props, makeup trailers, dressing rooms, security police, grips, production crews, actors…The place was teeming with professionals—and they were all there because I wrote some words on paper. It was overwhelming.

Quietly, I sat in my car for the longest of time and just watched. After years of being yesterday's news, I was page one of Variety and The Daily Reporter. The 'has-been' had arrived—torn car seat and all. A wave of emotion suddenly washed over me and I wished my parents were beside me, taking this all in. I could already hear my father nervously saying, 'Jesus Christ, how long are you gonna sit in the stupid car?' I laughed and cried at the same time. Relax, Dad, it's okay. I can sit here with my parents if I want. Your son, with the sneaky-but-lethal-left-hook—is the producer.

Photos

Christmas 1952 - Dad (Edward), me and Mom (Kitty)   *(Collection of the author)*

Me on the right - with neighbor kids on the stoop   *(Collection of the author)*

At CBS television studio   *(Collection of the author)*

With Danny Kaye - Inchworm number from the movie *Hans Christian Andersen*
(Collection of the author)

With Kirk Douglas from *The Juggler*   *(Collection of the author)*

(l. to r.) Edward Dmytryk, me and Kirk Douglas on the set of *The Juggler*
(Collection of the author)

Showing Edward Dmytryk that I can still juggle - on the set of *Anzio*
(Collection of the author)

(l. to r.) Robert Mitchum, me, Reni Santoni, Giancarlo Giannini, Peter Falk -
playing poker on the set of *Anzio*   *(Collection of the author)*

In *Anzio*   *(Collection of the author)*

289

In *Poltergeist*   *(Collection of the author)*

In *The Driver*   *(Collection of the author)*

With Gregory Peck in *Captain Newman, MD*   *(Collection of the author)*

With George Segal in *California Split*   *(Collection of the author)*

(l. to r.) George Segal, brother Ed, Mickey Fox, Elliott Gould in *California Split*
(Collection of the author)

Elliott Gould and George Segal in *California Split*   *(Collection of the author)*

(l. to r.) Me, sister-in-law, Dad, Robert Altman, Mom, Bert Remsen, Elliott Gould
(Collection of the author)

Lifelong friend, Elliott Gould

(Collection of the author)

(l. to r.) Agent Guy McElwaine, me and Alan Ladd, Jr. (Laddie) celebrating football win *(Collection of the author)*

Having some fun with Alan Ladd, Jr. (Laddie) on the set of *The Driver* *(Collection of the author)*

With my better half, wife Barbara Lightstone Walsh (Lights)   *Collection of the author)*

Addendum

In 1995, I was playing poker with Robert Finkelstein, an attorney, and at the dinner break the subject of Frank Sinatra came up. Finkelstein at that time, was working with Sinatra sorting out family royalties concerning Sinatra's music. So in a very casual way I told him my story concerning Sinatra. Working with him in early TV. Giving him the present of a tie. Seeing it left behind. The whole bit. He seemed quite amused by the story and we had a good laugh over it.

The following week Finkelstein shows up at the poker game with a present from Sinatra. It was a tie from his special collection, made with colors only used in Sinatra's paintings. Also a 24 Karat Gold CD of his concert THE SUMMIT, featuring Sinatra, Dean Martin, and Sammy Davis Jr., recorded live at The Villa Venice, Chicago. My surprise gift came with a note from Sinatra:

Dec. 5, 1995

Dear Joey,

Now it's my turn with a tie!! Enjoy!

Happy Holidays,

Frank Sinatra

It's been 25 years and I still haven't unwrapped the CD, nor worn the tie. I seem to be treating it like fine wine, as in the more it ages, the better the appreciation. Of course if Sinatra were still with us, he'd be saying...

"What's wrong with you...It's just an okay CD, and I got plenty of ties like that sucker, so get over it kid."

Made in the USA
Las Vegas, NV
02 May 2022